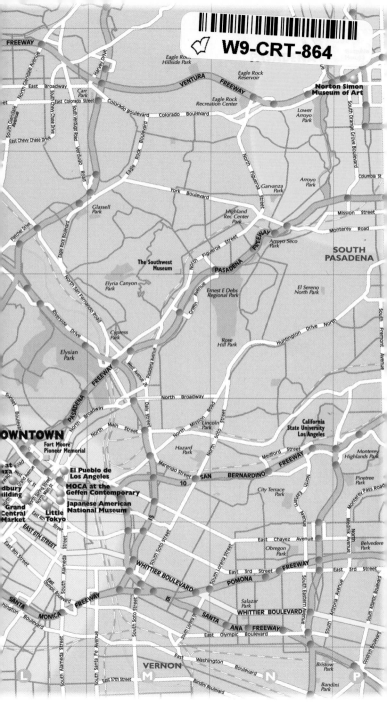

Fodor's

Los Angeles'
25Best

by Emma Stanford

Fodor's Travel Publications
New York • Toronto
London • Sydney • Auckland
www.fodors.com

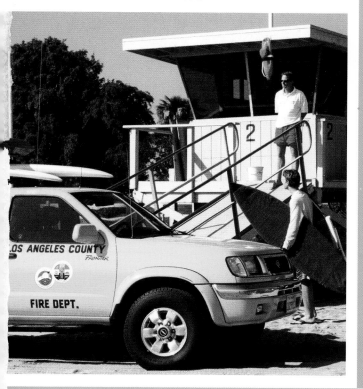

How to Use
This Book

KEY TO SYMBOLS

✚ Map reference to the accompanying fold-out map

✉ Address

☎ Telephone number

🕐 Opening/closing times

🍴 Restaurant or café

🚆 Nearest rail station

Ⓜ Nearest subway (Metro) station

🚌 Nearest bus route

⛴ Nearest riverboat or ferry stop

♿ Facilities for visitors with disabilities

❓ Other practical information

▷ Further information

ℹ Tourist information

✋ Admission charges: Expensive (over $11), Moderate ($6–$11), and Inexpensive ($6 or less)

★ Major Sight   ★ Minor Sight

👣 Walks   🚌 Excursions

🛍 Shops

🎵 Entertainment and Nightlife

🍴 Restaurants

This guide is divided into four sections

• Essential Los Angeles: an introduction to the city and tips on making the most of your stay.
• Los Angeles by Area: We've broken the city into five areas, and recommended the best sights, shops, entertainment venues, nightlife and restaurants in each one. Suggested walks help you to explore on foot.
• Where to Stay: the best hotels, whether you're looking for luxury, budget or something in between.
• Need to Know: the info you need to make your trip run smoothly, including getting about by public transport, weather tips, emergency phone numbers and useful websites.

Navigation In the Los Angeles by Area chapter, we've given each area its own color, which is also used on the locator maps throughout the book and the map on the inside front cover.

Maps The fold-out map accompanying this book is a comprehensive street plan of Los Angeles. The grid on this fold-out map is the same as the grid on the locator maps within the book. We've given grid references within the book for each sight and listing.

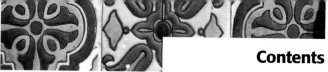

Contents

CONTENTS

Introducing Los Angeles

Squeezed into 4,752sq miles (12,308sq km), split by a mountain range and flanked by the Pacific Ocean, this megalopolis of more than 10 million people has been made famous by novels, movies, TV shows and—despite the smog—sunny weather.

Los Angeles is a magnet for immigrants, becoming in many respects the northernmost Latin American city and the eastern-most Asian city. And it is also a tremendous magnet for tourists.

Sprawling LA is often described as lacking an urban core, which is tough to dispute: visitors can't take in LA County by exploring just a few square miles. Time and energy are required, but the region rewards anyone who is willing to expend a bit of both.

Few cities match the enticements showcased here: gorgeous beaches, theme parks, world-class museums and theater, and glitzy celebrities and fashions. The city is as disparate and complex as the many writers who set their stories here, from Raymond Chandler and Robert Towne to Joan Didion and Walter Mosely.

For a visitor, this means that a trip to LA is a collection of experiences, each with a different feel and backstory. And the story is constantly changing, as many neighborhoods are enjoying resurgences, from back-to-its-glam-roots Hollywood to Culver City, with its celebrity chefs, art galleries and increasingly bustling nightlife. And other neighborhoods such as Santa Monica, Venice and Beverly Hills remain as popular and well visited as ever.

With all there is to do and see—including dining in hip restaurants, browsing in stylish stores and viewing priceless artwork—it's hard to slow down and let yourself slip into the southern California rhythm. But one thing is for sure: When you do, LA, with its laid-back ways (except in heavy traffic) will get under your skin, even if that skin isn't taut and tanned!

Facts + Figures

- LA has the tallest building between Chicago and Malaysia, the 1,018ft (310m) US Bank Tower.
- The city is home to nine Frank Lloyd Wright structures and more than a dozen by Frank Gehry, including the Hollywood Bowl.

WEALTHY ANGELENOS

Businessman and Beverly Hills resident Kirk Kerkorian tops the list of wealthiest Angelenos ($15 billion); Sumner Redstone, CEO of Viacom, comes in second ($8 billion); and movie mogul David Geffen ($4.7 billion) and director/producer Stephen Spielberg ($3 billion) both make the top ten.

WHAT'S IN A NAME?

Street and neighborhood names in Los Angeles are as varied as the city. Venice, with its canals and boardwalk, is a tribute to the Italian city, while Century City's moniker comes from the movie studio, 20th Century Fox. And busy Pico Boulevard was named for Pio Pico, "Alta" California's last governor.

NICKNAMES

Nicknames abound for Los Angeles, including the obvious LA, along with Lalaland, the Southland, the City of Angels, Lotusville, and El Pueblo ("the town" in Spanish). Folks from Hollywood might be called Hollywoodites, Hollywoodians, or Hollywooders. Anyone from Long Beach is simply a Long Beacher.

A Short Stay in Los Angeles

DAY 1

Morning Start your day at 8.30 with breakfast at **Brighton Coffee Shop** (▷ 46), an authentic 1950s spot that will provide much-needed energy for the busy day.

Mid-morning Shop on **Rodeo Drive** (▷ 26, 42), passing stores like Gucci, Versace and Dior. Many open at 10am, but don't worry if you're a bit early: You can spare your wallet by window-shopping.

Lunch Head to the **Getty Center** (▷ 70) for a quick lunch; if the sun is shining, choose the outdoor café.

Afternoon Spend two hours taking in the Getty Center's collections (don't miss the Old Masters, including works by Brueghel and Rembrandt), wandering around the grounds, and admiring the views of LA.

Mid-afternoon The morning fog has burned off, so make your way to the beach in **Santa Monica** (▷ 72–73). Rent a bicycle or Rollerblades and then zoom by the pier, Muscle Beach and the Venice boardwalk.

Dinner If you have time before dinner, enjoy a cocktail and the sunset at **Shutters on the Beach** (▷ 112) or **Veranda Bar at Casa del Mar** (▷ 82). Then have dinner at **Chinois on Main** (▷ 85), or another, more casual, restaurant on **Main Street** (▷ 79) in Santa Monica.

Evening After dinner, stroll the lively **Third Street Promenade** (▷ 80); there are a number of bars and live music venues in this area. If you're a moviegoer, consider catching an independent film at the **NuArt Theatre** (▷ 82), or opt for a mainstream choice at a Promenade theater.

DAY 2

Morning Start your day with a homey breakfast at 8.30 at the **Village Coffee Shop** (▷ 48) in Hollywood.

Mid-morning Wander down **Hollywood Boulevard** (▷ 30–31), traversing the Walk of Fame and passing Mann's Chinese Theatre. Climb the grand staircase in the **Hollywood and Highland** complex (▷ 41), next to Mann's, and take in the panoramic view of the Hollywood sign.

Lunch Head to **Greenblatt's** Jewish-style deli (▷ 47) on Sunset Boulevard in West Hollywood for a traditional corned-beef or pastrami sandwich.

Afternoon Visit the **Page Museum** (▷ 27) and **La Brea Tar Pits** (▷ 27) on the Miracle Mile stretch of Wilshire Boulevard. Don't let the smell of the tar pits turn you off from one of the world's most famous fossil sites. Some of the fossils are 40,000 years old.

Mid-afternoon For a different museum experience, head west on Wilshire for the **LA County Museum of Art** (▷ 32–33), which houses world-class collections ranging from ancient Asian and Egyptian art to 20th-century masters.

Dinner Treat yourself to California cuisine at **Lucques** (▷ 47) on Melrose, or dine in Beverly Hills at **Mr. Chow** (▷ 47), an LA institution.

Evening Take in a comedy show at **The Improv** (▷ 44), which has launched big-name comics and sometimes has surprise guests; or have a drink with the industry crowd at Bar Marmont, **Winston's** (▷ 45) or **The Standard** (▷ 45).

Top 25

► ► ►

The Arboretum of LA County ▷ **90** Lovely gardens in the San Gabriel Mountains.

Venice Beach ▷ **74–75** California's "Bohemia-by-the-sea," where there's always something going on.

Universal Studios Hollywood ▷ **34–35** The ultimate movie theme park will get the adrenalin rushing.

UCLA Hammer Museum ▷ **76** Welcome respite from the city's larger museums.

Santa Monica and Malibu ▷ **72–73** The seaside town of Santa Monica and California's premier surfing destination, Malibu, are hot spots.

Rancho Los Alamitos ▷ **103** Historic ranch with adobe house and lovely gardens.

El Pueblo de Los Angeles ▷ **59** The vibrant sights and sounds of old Mexico around Olvera Street.

Barnsdall Art Park and Hollyhock House ▷ **24** Visit Frank Lloyd Wright's first building.

Beverly Hills ▷ **25** Taste the American Dream in the glitziest part of LA.

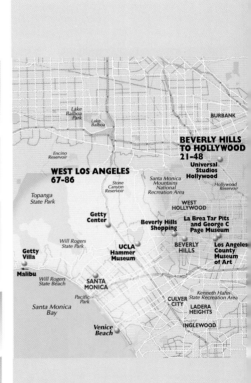

Norton Simon Museum of Art ▷ **94** Beautiful paintings and famous sculptures.

Natural History Museum ▷ **58** Everything you want to know about the history of the earth.

Museum of Contemporary Art ▷ **56–57** Interesting building, great modern art.

These pages are a quick guide to the Top 25, which are described in more detail later. Here they are listed alphabetically, and the tinted background shows which area they are in.

Shopping in Beverly Hills ▷ **26** The place to come for (window-) shopping and celebrity-spotting.

La Brea Tar Pits and Page Museum ▷ **27** LA's prehistoric creatures encased in tar.

Disneyland Resort ▷ **100–101** The world's first and most famous theme park repays a visit.

Gamble House ▷ **91** A luxurious example of early 20th-century architecture.

Getty Center ▷ **70** One of the world's most important cultural collections.

Getty Villa ▷ **71** The Getty's classical collections housed in a Roman villa.

Grand Central Market ▷ **52–53** Downtown's biggest indoor market.

Griffith Park and Observatory ▷ **28–29** Rolling acres of chaparral-clad hills that make a great escape from the city.

Hollywood Boulevard ▷ **30–31** The Hollywood and Highland shopping complex has brought glitz back to Hollywood Boulevard.

The Huntington ▷ **92–93** Library, art collection and botanical garden in one place.

Long Beach and the Queen Mary ▷ **102** There's a brilliant aquarium here as well as the old liner.

Little Tokyo ▷ **54–55** Japan meets downtown LA—interesting sights and peaceful gardens.

LA County Museum of Art ▷ **32–33** The best and most extensive art collection in LA.

Map labels:
Hahamongna Watershed Park
Brand Park
GLENDALE
ALTADENA
PASADENA 87-96
SIERRA MADRE
Gamble House
PASADENA
Brookside Park
Norton Simon Museum of Art
Arboretum of LA County
The Huntington
EAST PASADENA
SAN MARINO
Botanical Gardens
TEMPLE CITY
Griffith Park
Griffith Observatory
Hollywood Boulevard
Hollyhock House
Barnsdall Park
SOUTH PASADENA
EAST SAN GABRIEL
SAN GABRIEL
Ernest E Debs Regional Park
ALHAMBRA
Elysian Park
LOS ANGELES
El Pueblo de Los Angeles
MOCA at the Geffen Contemporary
Grand Central Market
Little Tokyo
ROSEMEAD
SOUTH SAN GABRIEL
EAST LOS ANGELES
Natural History Museum of LA County
VERNON
MONTEBELLO
Exposition Park
DOWNTOWN 49-66
PICO RIVERA
MAYWOOD
COMMERCE
BELL
FLORENCE-GRAHAM
CUDAHY
DOWNEY

Shopping

In this city where car is king, the ultimate purchase may be a custom vehicle, perhaps an impeccably restored Bentley or Excalibur, or a hand-painted flower-power Volkswagen bus. Still this is not the usual afternoon's shopping spree purchase.

Fashion

In this fashion-conscious (and, occasionally, fashion victim) city, almost everyone wants to be decked out in trendy clothing and costly jewels, especially if a hip restaurant or nightclub is on the agenda or a trip past a scrutinizing doorman is in the picture. And as you search among the city's hot boutiques for that special something that will get you from a yoga class to an Oscar party, you may well spot a celebrity or two.

Something from Rodeo Drive or Melrose Avenue is de rigueur–you'll find everything from mass-produced imports and hard-to-find vintage wear to pricey one-of-a-kind designs and jewelry, cool clubwear, shoes, bags, and other accessories. Though, not surprisingly, many of these creations come with sky-high price tags; it's nonetheless possible to waltz out of the door with some bauble or bangle you can actually afford.

Leisure Gear

However, it's not the high life and the beautiful people that draw all visitors to LA; many come for its enviable climate and myriad sports activities. Considering this combination, it's not surprising that sports equipment, surfboards,

LA is a shopper's paradise, with everything from designer stores to food markets

---

GRAB THE GLITZ

It's probably not a good idea to pry up a cement block of John Wayne's footprints at Mann's Chinese Theatre, like Lucille Ball did in an episode of *I Love Lucy*, but there are plenty of other movie-memorabilia souvenirs available. Hollywood Boulevard is lined with stores that sell movie-related T-shirts, baseball caps, shot glasses, water globes, key chains, posters, coffee mugs and other items.

skateboards, Rollerblades and a mind-boggling array of T-shirts, swimsuits, wetsuits, athletic wear and running shoes in a wide range of prices can be found all over town. Tennis and golf gear are also best sellers, and you will find something suitable for hitting the court or course, whether you play in a public park or a fancy country club.

House and Garden
You will also find a broad selection of quirky and high-end housewares. Angelenos, as fashion conscious about their homes and gardens as they are about their bodies, have assured a brisk business for purveyors of decorative items.

Music
Music is big business in the city. Humongous stores on the Sunset Strip and smaller specialized shops sell a dizzying range of new and used CDs that showcase every type of music, and associated merchandise, under the sun.

Books
From small shops to big retail chains, book-stores are plentiful here. Some focus on specialized interests such as cooking, mystery novels or cinema, whereas others offer a wide variety. You'll find bookstores everywhere, but look for clusters of them on Third Street in West Hollywood, on Hollywood Boulevard and in Westwood Village.

Many stores have doormen so smart dress is essential if you want to go in

---

MY BODY IS A TEMPLE

Health and body-conscious Los Angeles seduces shoppers with a multitude of products to soothe and beautify. Luxury spas and salons, as well as budget shops and flea markets, offer avocado facials, aromatherapy oils, hand-milled soaps and facelifts in a bottle. This regime, naturally, extends itself to food and drink—natural foods, nutritional supplements and soy meat products are easy to find throughout the region.

Shopping by Theme

Whether you're looking for a department store, a quirky boutique, or something in between, you'll find it all in Los Angeles. On this page shops are listed by theme. For a more detailed write-up, see the individual listings in Los Angeles by Area.

ART AND ANTIQUES

Antiquarius (▷ 40)
Bergamot Station (▷ 79)
Broadway Gallery Complex
   (▷ 79)
Casa de Sousa (▷ 63)
Cirrus Gallery (▷ 63)
Del Mano Gallery (▷ 79)
Gemini G.E.L. (▷ 40)
Louis Stern Fine Arts
   (▷ 41)
Margo Leavin Gallery
   (▷ 41)
Santa Monica Outdoor
   Antiques and
   Collectable Market
   (▷ 80)

BOOKS AND MUSIC

Amoeba Music (▷ 40)
Bodhi Tree (▷ 40)
Book Soup (▷ 40)
Borders Books and Music
   (▷ 79)
Canterbury Records
   (▷ 95)
A Different Light (▷ 40)
Every Picture Tells a Story
   (▷ 79)
Hear Music (▷ 79)
Small World Books & the
   Mystery Annexe (▷ 80)
Vroman's (▷ 95)

MEN'S AND WOMEN'S CLOTHING

The Blue Jeans Bar (▷ 79)
Fred Segal (▷ 40, 79)
Frederick's of Hollywood
   (▷ 40)
Jay Wolf (▷ 41)
Lisa Kline (▷ 41)
Maxfield's (▷ 41)
Prada (▷ 42)

MOVIE MEMORABILIA

Hollywood Boulevard
   (▷ 41)
Larry Edmunds' Bookshop
   (▷ 41)
Samuel French Theater &
   Film Bookshop (▷ 42)
Vidiots (▷ 80)

RETRO AND SECOND-HAND CLOTHING

Aardvarks (▷ 40)
American Rag (▷ 40)
Freaks (▷ 63)
Gotta Have It (▷ 79)
It's a Wrap (▷ 41)
Paris 1900 (▷ 80)
Wasteland (▷ 42)

SHOPPING DISTRICTS

505 Flower (▷ 63)
Abbot Kinney Boulevard
   (▷ 79)
Chung King Road (▷ 63)
Main Street (▷ 79)
Melrose Avenue (▷ 41)
Montana Avenue (▷ 79)
Mission Street (▷ 95)
Old Town Pasadena
   (▷ 95)
Rodeo Drive (▷ 42)
Santee Alley (▷ 63)
South Lake Avenue (▷ 95)
Sunset Plaza (▷ 42)
Third Street Promenade
   (▷ 80)
Westwood Village (▷ 80)

SHOPPING MALLS

Beverly Center (▷ 40)
The Grove at Farmers
   Market (▷ 40)
Hollywood and Highland
   (▷ 41)
Santa Monica Place (▷ 80)
Seventh & Fig (▷ 63)
Universal City Walk (▷ 42)
Westfield Century City
   (▷ 80)
Westside Pavilion (▷ 80)

SPECIALTY SHOPS

Flower Mart (▷ 63)
LA Eyeworks (▷ 41)
McManus and Morgan
   (▷ 63)
Plastica (▷ 42)
The Puzzle Zoo (▷ 80)
Soolip Paperie & Press
   (▷ 42)
St. Vincent Jewelry Center
   (▷ 63)
Wacko (▷ 42)
Wanna Buy a Watch?
   (▷ 42)

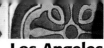

Los Angeles by Night

In Los Angeles, the undisputed entertainment capital of the world, the hardest part of planning a night on the town is choosing among the many diverse and eclectic options.

Clubs and Cinemas

West Hollywood's Sunset Strip has been a perennial favorite for night-clubbers since the city's Golden Era. Visitors and locals alike are still bedazzled by such venerable venues as Whisky A Go Go, the Viper Room, the Roxy and the Comedy Store, as well as nostalgic bars, hip clubs and Tinseltown's most magnificent cinemas such as Mann's, the vintage Pantages and the Kodak Theatre.

Where to Go

In Santa Monica and on the Westside—other good places for an evening out—the pedestrian-only Third Street Promenade bustles with open-air cafés, celebrity-haunt bars, street musicians and entertainers; the people-watching is some of the best in town. Downtown's showpiece Performing Arts Center, which houses the Walt Disney Concert Hall, hosts major theatrical performances and is the seasonal home of the Los Angeles Philharmonic Orchestra, the Los Angeles Opera and the Los Angeles Master Chorale. Other venues throughout the city present a delightful range of theatrical works, and you often spot well-known talents both on stage and in the audience.

STARRY NIGHT

Because of the city's mild year-round climate, most Angelenos like being outdoors whenever possible, even after dark. For years, residents have flocked to the Hollywood Bowl to enjoy summer concert series such as the Playboy Jazz Festival, seasonal performances by the LA Philharmonic Orchestra and a lengthy list of international talents. Part of the fun is packing a picnic to enjoy under the stars. Griffith Park's Greek Theater is more intimate. And beach parties, all along the coast, never go out of style.

Los Angeles has something to entertain everyone; choose from cocktails, jazz, theater and more

Eating Out

Angelenos have a passionate interest in wining and dining—it's no accident that this is where the term "foodie" originated. There are inevitably many places where you would go primarily to see and be seen, but these are still outnumbered by a huge assortment of casual cafés and take-out stalls. And in this most casual of cities, you rarely need to worry about the dress code.

What to Eat

With a diverse population, ethnic cuisine of all kinds is available almost everywhere in LA. The mild climate means fresh produce is abundant, and is incorporated into most menus. There is an exceptionally large choice for vegetarians and the health-conscious.

Where to Eat

Third Street Promenade is packed with restaurants and cafés, while the Venice Boardwalk is the place to try something unusual (and inexpensive). There are pricey seafood restaurants along the Pacific Coast Highway. In Beverly Hills you will need to have a larger budget and dress up a little, although the nearby student area of Westwood is less glamorous. The large Hollywood and Highland complex has all manner of dining outlets, while trendy stars and restaurants cluster around Melrose Avenue. Downtown has large hotels and old Pasadena specializes in bistros and cafés.

PRICES AND MEAL TIMES

Except for luxury restaurants, where dinner could easily cost upward of $70 for two people excluding wine (lunch will be less; typically around $40), dining in LA need not cost an arm and a leg. If you eat in reasonable restaurants, anticipate spending around $8–$10 per person for breakfast, $10–$12 for lunch and $15–$20 for dinner excluding drinks. Wherever you dine, a tip of at least 15 percent of the check is expected. Angelenos generally have lunch between 11.30 and 2, and dinner between 6 and 9, but many restaurants open earlier and close later.

Even the fussiest of eaters will find something they like in LA

Restaurants by Cuisine

There are restaurants to suit all tastes and budgets in Los Angeles. On this page they are listed by cuisine. For a more detailed description of each restaurant, see Los Angeles by Area.

ASIAN

Chin Chin (▷ 46)
Crustacean (▷ 46)
Electric Lotus (▷ 47)
Empress Pavilion (▷ 66)
The Hump (▷ 85)
Katsuya (▷ 85)
Mandarin Deli (▷ 66)
Mr. Chow (▷ 47)
Saladang Song (▷ 96)
Seoul Jung (▷ 66)
Thousand Cranes (▷ 66)
Yujean Kang's (▷ 96)

CAFÉS, DELIS AND SNACKS

Apple Pan (▷ 85)
Barney Greengrass (▷ 46)
La Brea Bakery (▷ 46)
Brighton Coffee Shop (▷ 46)
Canter's (▷ 46)
Doughboys (▷ 46)
Greenblatt's (▷ 47)
Kokomo (▷ 47)
Newsroom Café (▷ 48)
Original Pantry Café (▷ 66)
Philippe the Original (▷ 66)
Pink's Famous Chili Dogs (▷ 48)
Rose Café (▷ 86)
Sidewalk Café (▷ 86)
Village Coffee Shop (▷ 48)
World Café (▷ 86)

CALIFORNIA CUISINE

The Belvedere (▷ 46)
Chaya (▷ 46)
Checker's (▷ 66)
Chinois on Main (▷ 85)
Ford's Filling Station (▷ 85)
Lucques (▷ 47)
Michael's (▷ 86)
One Pico (▷ 86)
Parkway Grill (▷ 96)
The Raymond (▷ 96)
Restaurant at the Getty Center (▷ 86)
Spago Beverly Hills (▷ 48)

FRENCH

Bistro 45 (▷ 96)
La Cachette (▷ 85)
Ortolan (▷ 48)
Patina (▷ 66)
Twin Palms (▷ 96)

ITALIAN

Drago (▷ 85)
Fritto Misto (▷ 85)
Locanda Veneta (▷ 47)
Mi Piace (▷ 96)
Valentino (▷ 86)

MEXICAN AND SOUTHWESTERN

Border Grill (▷ 85)
El Cholo (▷ 46)
La Golondrina (▷ 66)
Maria Tex Mex Playa (▷ 86)
Mexico City (▷ 47)
La Serenata Gourmet (▷ 86)
Sonora Café (▷ 48)
El Torito Grill (▷ 48)

MISCELLANEOUS

Figtree (▷ 85)
Gordon Biersch Brewery (▷ 96)
Inn of the 7th Ray (▷ 85)
Luna Park (▷ 47)
Off Vine (▷ 48)
Trader Vic's (▷ 48)
Versailles (▷ 86)

STEAK, SEAFOOD AND HEARTY FARE

Arroyo Chop House (▷ 96)
The Ivy (▷ 47)
Lawry's the Prime Rib (▷ 47)
Morton's (▷ 47)
Musso & Frank Grill (▷ 48)
Pacific Dining Car (▷ 66)
Palm Restaurant (▷ 48)
Saddle Peak Lodge (▷ 86)
Water Grill (▷ 66)

If You Like...

However you'd like to spend your time in Los Angeles, these top suggestions should help you tailor your ideal visit. Each sight or listing has a fuller write-up in Los Angeles by Area.

DESIGNER LABELS

Visit the Fred Segal stores in Santa Monica (▷ 79) and on Melrose (▷ 40).
Head to Montana Avenue (▷ 79) in Santa Monica for boutique shopping.
Meander along Rodeo Drive (▷ 26, 42) for the high-end retail experience.

FUNKY AND UNUSUAL FINDS

Try on vintage clothes at Aardvarks (▷ 40).
Visit Chung King Road (▷ 63) and Olvera Street (▷ 59) in Downtown.
Check out antiques on Abbot Kinney (▷ 79).
Pop into a gallery in Santa Monica's Bergamot Station (▷ 79).

Los Angeles has designer stores and more unusual shops (above)

A HEARTY MEAL IN THE MORNING

Fill up at Kokomo's (▷ 47) in the Farmer's Market.
Nibble on delicious bread and pastries at Doughboys (▷ 46).
Dine Downtown at ex-mayor Riordan's Original Pantry Café (▷ 66).
Splurge on a hotel brunch at Shutters (▷ 112) or the Beverly Wilshire (▷ 112).

DISTINCT ARCHITECTURE

See a show at Frank Gehry's Walt Disney Concert Hall (▷ Music Center, 64).
Stroll around the grounds of the Getty Center (▷ 70).
Visit Hollyhock House (▷ 24), LA's most famous Frank Lloyd Wright structure.

The Beverly Wilshire hotel (above right); the Getty Center (right)

Casual café fare;
Santa Monica (below)

OUTDOOR EATS

Wait in line for a hot dog at Pink's Famous Chili Dogs (▷ 48).

Have a casual meal at Rose Café (▷ 86) in Venice.

Dine on California cuisine at The Raymond (▷ 96) or Off Vine (▷ 48).

SLEEPING NEAR THE OCEAN

Stick to a tight budget at Bayside Hotel (▷ 109) in Santa Monica.

Spend time near the Santa Monica Pier at Best Western Ocean View Hotel (▷ 110).

Unwind at Channel Road Inn Bed and Breakfast (▷ 110), a Colonial Revival house.

Luxuriate at Shutters (▷ 112), a New England-style hotel on the beach.

FUN IN THE SUN

Enjoy an afternoon concert at the Hollywood Bowl (▷ 44).

Visit the Arboretum of LA County (▷ 90).

Hop on a trolley tour of Beverly Hills (▷ 25).

Learn how to surf from an expert (▷ 83).

Take a gondola ride in Long Beach after a visit to the *Queen Mary* (▷ 102).

Learning to surf (above)

A NIGHT OUT

See an old film at Silent Movie Theater, the last theater in the US to show silent films (▷ 45).

Traverse the universe at a show in Griffith Observatory's planetarium (▷ 28–29).

Hear live music at McCabe's Guitar Shop (▷ 82).

Griffith Park and Observatory (left)

SAVING YOUR PENNIES

Visit LACMA (▷ 32–33) after 5pm, when admission is free.
Saunter down Hollywood Boulevard and the Walk of Fame (▷ 30–31).
Hike in Topanga Canyon (▷ 77).
Rest your head at the friendly, inexpensive Farmer's Daughter (▷ 109).

Hollywood Walk of Fame and Spago (below)

LIVING THE HIGH LIFE

Enjoy a massage at Thibiant European Day Spa (▷ 45) or Burke Williams Day Spa (▷ 81).
Have tea at the Peninsula Beverly Hills (▷ 112).
Bet on horses at Santa Anita Race Track (▷ 95).
Dine at Ortolan (▷ 48), Patina (▷ 66) or Spago Beverly Hills (▷ 48).

YOUR KIDS

Rent a two-seater bike at the beach (▷ 74–75).
Ride the Ferris wheel at the Santa Monica Pier (▷ 72–73).
Spend time with Mickey and friends at Disneyland (▷ 100–101).
Entertain the family at Universal Studios (▷ 34–35) and Knott's Berry Farm (▷ 104).
See skeletons and fossilized remains at La Brea Tar Pits and Page Museum (▷ 27).

Your kids will enjoy La Brea Tar Pits and Page Museum (above)

CELEB SPOTTING

Relax with celebrities at the Ivy on Robertson (▷ 47).
Get on the guest list at Hyde Lounge (▷ 44).
Reserve a spot on the Warner Brothers Studio VIP tour (▷ 38).

Spot celebs at Warner Brothers Studios (right)

ESSENTIAL LOS ANGELES **IF YOU LIKE...**

FEB 7TH 1938

To
id Grauman
with every
good wish

Nelson Eddy

DEC 28 38

d boy
am happy to
t my foot in it for you

Bill Powell

10-20-36

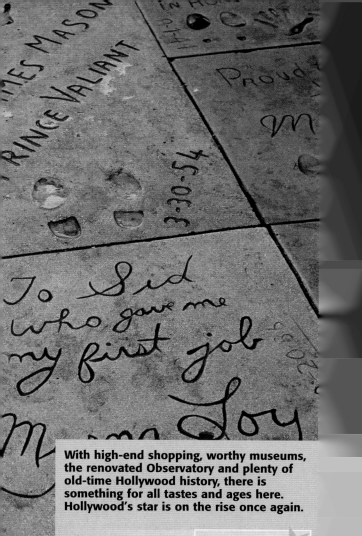

To Sid who gave me my first job

With high-end shopping, worthy museums, the renovated Observatory and plenty of old-time Hollywood history, there is something for all tastes and ages here. Hollywood's star is on the rise once again.

VENTURA

Riverside Drive

West Riverside Drive

Weddington Park North

Toluca Lake

101

Weddington Park South

Cahuenga Boulevard West

Universal Studios Hollywood

Tujunga Avenue

Laurel Canyon Boulevard

Mulholland Drive

Laurel Canyon Park

Mulholland Drive

Mulholland Drive

Mulholland Drive

Cahuenga Boulevard

Hollywood Heritage Museum

Santa Monica Mountains National Recreation Area

Coldwater Canyon Drive

Wattles Garden Park

Runyon Canyon Park

Ripley's Believe It or Not

Hollywood Roosevelt Hotel

Virginia Robinson Mansion and Gardens

Greystone Park

WEST HOLLYWOOD

Plummer Park

SANTA MONICA

Egyptian Theater

North Fairfax Avenue

North La Brea Avenue

Holloway Drive

West Sunset Boulevard

Museum of Contemporary Art (satellite gallery)

North La Cienega Boulevard

Melrose Avenue

La Brea Avenue

Museum of Television and Radio

North Beverly Drive

Beverly Boulevard

Pan Pacific Park

La Brea Tar Pits and George C Page Museum

South Beverly Drive

SANTA MONICA BOULEVARD

Burton Way

Los Angeles County Museum of Art

Craft and Folk Art Museum

Beverly Hills Shopping

Wilshire Boulevard

Museum of the Holocaust

La Cienega Park

BEVERLY HILLS

Petersen Automotive Museum

Wilshire Boulevard

Boulevard

SANTA MONICA

West Olympic Boulevard

La Cienega Boulevard

San Vicente Boulevard

West Olympic Boulevard

Museum of Tolerance

West Olympic Boulevard

South Robertson Boulevard

South La Cienega Boulevard

South Fairfax Avenue

Cheviot Hills Park and Recreation Center

2

3

4

5

6

7

F

G

H

Barnsdall Art Park/ Hollyhock House

The concrete-and-stucco Hollyhock House, designed by Frank Lloyd Wright

THE BASICS

www.hollyhockhouse.net
www.barnsdallartpark.com
⊞ K5
✉ Barnsdall Art Park, 4800 Hollywood Boulevard, Hollywood
☎ 323/644-6269
🕐 Tours Wed–Sun 12.30, 1.30, 2.30, 3.30 (reservations required)
🚇 Metro Red Line
💰 Inexpensive

HIGHLIGHTS

● Hollyhock House interior
● Views over Hollywood from Barnsdall Art Park
● Free summer Shakespeare performances

LA's architectural treasure was designed by Frank Lloyd Wright. Visitors can explore the bold lines of Hollyhock House and view local artists' work in the gallery on the grounds.

Hollyhock House When unconventional millionaire oil heiress Aline Barnsdall arrived in Los Angeles in 1915 from Chicago she intended to found a theatrical community. She bought a 36-acre (15ha) site called Olive Hill, on the eastern side of Hollywood, and commissioned architect Frank Lloyd Wright to design the project. The full plan was never realized because of artistic and financial differences, but the residence was completed. The concrete-and-stucco building, which has a square shape reminiscent of pre-Columbian architecture, was named Hollyhock House after Aline Barnsdall's favorite flower, and stylized hollyhocks decorate the building inside and out.

Neglect and renovation Barnsdall gave the property to the city in 1927 for use as a public art park. It was altered over the years as different tenants used it, and earthquakes and weather also took their toll. It was designated a national monument in 1963, but only in 2000 was it shut down for a thorough restoration.

Art park The grounds officially reopened as Barnsdall Art Park in 2003. It contains the Los Angeles Municipal Gallery, which displays works by local and international artists, and the Gallery Theater, where local groups stage performances.

Beverly Hills

The Hollywood sign was erected in 1923 to advertise a residential development (right)

You can't say you've "done LA" until you've seen Beverly Hills. The city's most recognizable ZIP code (90210) is also LA's most visited neighborhood, receiving over 14 million visitors a year.

A star is born In a classic rags-to-riches story, the countrified suburb of Beverly Hills, west of Hollywood, was plucked from obscurity by movie stars—Douglas Fairbanks Jr. set up home here in 1919, followed by Charlie Chaplin, Gloria Swanson and Rudolph Valentino.

Seeing the sights Historical Beverly Hills walking tour maps are available from the Visitors Bureau. The walk takes about two hours and covers such local sights as the imposing City Hall (▷ 61), Beverly Gardens and the wonderful Gaudí-like O'Neill House at No. 507 N. Rodeo Drive (go down the alley to admire the swirling stucco and mosaic inlay of the guest house). If you want to see movie moguls at play, try the Polo Lounge at the flamingo-pink Beverly Hills Hotel (▷ 112). To watch a television program or listen to a radio show from the 1920s to the present day, visit the Museum of Television and Radio (▷ 37).

Wide-open spaces With so many gorgeous mansions in the area, it's no surprise that Beverly Hills is also home to exquisite gardens. Greystone Park (▷ 36) offers views of the city, while the estate of Virginia Robinson (tours by appointment only, ▷ 38), which is on the National Register of Historic Places, features tropical flowers and plants.

THE BASICS

➕ G6

Beverly Hills Visitors Bureau
www.lovebeverlyhills.org
✉ 239 S. Beverly Drive
☎ 310/248-1015; 800/345-2210
🕐 Mon–Fri 8.30–5
🚌 14, 21

Beverly Hills Trolley Tour
✉ Rodeo Drive/Dayton Way
☎ 310/285-2438
🕐 Hourly departures Sat 11–4; extended hours in summer and during hols (Note: trolleys do not operate in the rain). Tour duration 40 minutes
✋ Moderate

HIGHLIGHTS

● People-watching in the Golden Triangle
● Brunch or a cocktail at a luxury hotel

Shopping in Beverly Hills

TOP 25

Designer stores abound on Rodeo Drive in Beverly Hills

THE BASICS

www.lovebeverlyhills.org
www.beverlyhillschamber.com
🚇 F6
🚌 4, 14, 21
♿ Good
❓ Check website for a list of retailers in Beverly Hills

HIGHLIGHTS

● Two Rodeo retail complex
● Prada Beverly Hills (No. 343) designed by Rem Koolhaas
● Perusing the art galleries

TIPS

● Robertson Boulevard, several blocks east of the Golden Triangle, also has great boutiques for menswear, womenswear and home decor.
● Some boutiques are closed on Sunday.

Beverly Hills remains ostentatiously star-studded. For black-belt window shopping, there's the Golden Triangle, bounded by Crescent Drive and Wilshire and Santa Monica boulevards, and bisected by world-famous Rodeo Drive, a showpiece three-block strip of designer emporiums.

Two Rodeo At the Wilshire Boulevard end, the $200-million self-proclaimed "European-style" Two Rodeo fashion retail complex is built around Via Rodeo Cobblestone Walkway (which dates from 1914), complete with a miniaturized version of Rome's Spanish Steps. It is lined with individually designed exclusive stores, including the busiest branch of jewelers Tiffany & Co. outside Manhattan, Versace and Gucci Fine Jewelry.

Rodeo Drive The other "mall" on Rodeo, the Rodeo Collection, all old brick and rose marble, lies up the street at No. 421. It has five levels filled with slightly less stellar brands. In between the two malls, the Rodeo sidewalks are lined with familiar international brands such as Van Cleef & Arpels (No. 300), Louis Vuitton (No. 295) and Giorgio Beverly Hills (No. 327). Many of these stores have doormen, so you will have to look the part if you actually want to go in.

Off Rodeo Drive The side streets off Rodeo Drive offer less expensive and well-known options. Beverly Drive has retail chains like Banana Republic, Ann Taylor and Williams-Sonoma, while Brighton Way has trendy retailers.

La Brea Tar Pits and Page Museum

A model mammoth (left) and a reconstructed skeleton (right)

It's hard to imagine in the conurbation of today, but during the last Ice Age the Los Angeles Basin teemed with wolves, saber-toothed cats and mammoths. Proof of their presence is in their bones, more than a million of which have been interred precisely where they died, in the primal black ooze of La Brea Tar Pits.

The pits Oozing from a fissure in the earth's crust, these gooey black tar pits (*brea* is Spanish for tar) are one of the world's most famous fossil sites. For thousands of years during the last great Ice Age, plants, birds and animals have been trapped and entombed here, turning the asphalt into a paleontological soup from which scientists have recovered millions of fossilized remnants from some 420 species of animal and 140 types of plant. Most of the fossils date from 10,000 to 40,000 years ago. The pits are fenced in and are attractive neither to look at nor to smell, but they are surrounded by pleasant Hancock Park, where you can stroll and picnic.

George C. Page Museum The museum opened in 1977 to provide explanation and context to the bones and fossils pulled out of the pits. Here you can see reconstructed skeletons of extinct species like saber-toothed tigers and giant sloths. There is also a short film about the history of the digs—excavation dates back to 1906—and a Paleontology Laboratory, where visitors can watch scientists in action cleaning and classifying the uncovered bones.

THE BASICS

www.tarpits.org

🏳 H6

✉ The George C. Page Museum at the La Brea Tar Pits, 5801 Wilshire Boulevard, Midtown

☎ 323/934-7243

🕐 Mon–Fri 9.30–5, Sat–Sun 10–5. Guided tours of tar pits daily at 1, of museum daily at 2.15 (volunteer guides permitting). Closed national hols

🚌 20, 21, 22, 217

♿ Good

✋ Moderate

HIGHLIGHT

● Model of a trapped mammoth in Lake Pit

TIP

● Pit 91 is still full of buried fossils, and excavation continues for about two months every summer, when you can watch the paleontologists at work from the observation area.

Griffith Park and Observatory

NEWTON
1642 – 1727

KEPLER
1571 – 1630

A vast open-air park straddling the Hollywood Hills, Griffith Park offers a raft of activities, the Museum of the American West and, from its landmark Observatory, the best view of the Hollywood sign.

A handsome bequest The largest municipal park in the United States, Griffith Park lies in the foothills of the Santa Monica Mountains. The original 3,015-acre (1,220ha) site was given to the city in 1896 by Col. Griffith Jenkins Griffith, who also left a trust with sufficient funds to build the amphitheater-style Greek Theater in 1930, a favorite outdoor concert venue, and the Griffith Observatory, which overlooks the city and houses an astronomy museum. The Observatory includes the Reiss telescope, freestanding telescopes and laser shows at the Samuel Oschin Planetarium

A monument to notable scientists in Griffith Park (far left); statue of movie star James Dean (middle); cycling through the park (bottom left); view of LA from the Griffith Observatory (bottom middle); the black dome of the Observatory (bottom right); aerial view of the park (right)

(▷ 35). Sharing cultural space in the park is the Museum of the American West, which was co-founded by actor Gene Autry and explores the West's influence on the world.

Around the park The park offers a tremendous variety of scenery. You can walk the cool, leafy Ferndell trail or reach the rugged high chaparral by a network of trails and easy-to-follow fire roads (maps from the Ranger Station). In the southeast corner of the park, near the Los Feliz exit, there are miniature train rides and children's pony rides. The antique merry-go-round, near the central Ranger Station, is adored by small children, and there are picnic areas, 28 tennis courts and four golf courses with plenty of parking nearby. Farther north, the Los Angeles Zoo (▷ 37) has 1,200 animals on 77 landscaped acres (31ha).

THE BASICS

➕ J4
✉ Off I–5/Golden State Freeway and 134/Ventura Freeway in the north
☎ Ranger Station: 323/913-4688. Observatory: 213/473-0890. Equestrian Center: 818/840-9063
🕐 Daily 6am–10pm (trails and mountain roads close at sunset). Observatory: Tue–Fri 12–10, Sat–Sun 10–10. Merry-go-round: weekends 11–5, daily in summer. Miniature train rides: daily 10–4.30 (until 5 weekends and hols). Pony rides: Tue–Sun 10–5
🍴 Refreshment stands
🚌 96
♿ Observatory: good. Park: good to nonexistent
✋ Observatory: moderate. Fees for other attractions, including planetarium

Hollywood Boulevard

**Though Hollywood Boulevard's 1930s
and 1940s heyday is a distant memory,
the Hollywood and Highland complex
and the return of the Academy Awards
have put some of the glitz back.**

Facelift After 50 years of decay and decline,
Tinseltown's most evocative address is undergoing
a major facelift. One of the first things to be
buffed up has been the corner of Hollywood
Boulevard and Highland Avenue. Next to Mann's
Chinese Theatre, the Hollywood and Highland
(▷ 41) five-floor, open-air retail and entertainment
complex bedazzles with its fine stores, restaurants
and a grand staircase that leads to a panoramic
view of the Hollywood sign. The 3,500-seat Kodak
Theatre is now the home for the Academy Awards
ceremony. Everyone is invited to place their hands,

Crocodile Dundee and Marilyn Monroe lookalikes (far left); Ripley's Believe it or Not! (bottom far left); novelty license plates for sale (bottom left); neon signs (bottom middle); wall mural depicting Hollywood stars (bottom right); the Walk of Fame (middle); masks decorating Mann's Chinese Theatre (right)

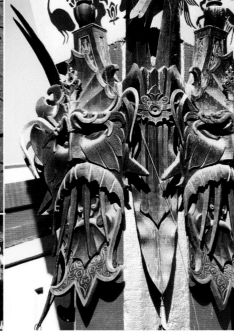

feet, hooves or (in the case of Betty Grable) legs in those of the stars, in the concrete courtyard of Mann's Chinese Theatre. Booths sell self-guiding Hollywood star site maps, although they're not always accurate.

Hollywood history Sid Grauman, who built the Chinese Theatre, was also one of the founding partners in the Hollywood Roosevelt Hotel (▷ 37, 111) across the street. A couple of Michelle Pfeiffer's nightclub scenes from *The Fabulous Baker Boys* (1989) were filmed here. The Capitol Records Tower (▷ 36) is a famous landmark. An assortment of celebrity figures can be found in the Hollywood Wax Museum at 6767 Hollywood Boulevard, while kids might enjoy the Hollywood Guinness World of Records Museum (▷ 36).

THE BASICS

✠ J5

Visitor Information Center

www.lacvb.com

✉ Hollywood and Highland Complex

☎ 323/467-6412

🕐 Mon–Sat 10–10, Sun 10–7

🚌 180, 181, 212, 217

Ⓜ Metro Red Line

♿ Free

LA County Museum of Art

HIGHLIGHTS

- Drawings by Degas
- *Edo* scrolls and *netsuke*, Japanese Pavilion
- Paintings and drawings by Kandinsky and Rodchenko
- *La Pipe*, Magritte
- Persian illuminated manuscripts
- *Untitled*, Rothko
- *Waterlilies*, Monet

TIP

- LACMA is undergoing expansion, including a new building for contemporary art.

One of the finest, most broad-ranging art museums in the United States, LACMA also stages alfresco jazz concerts and chamber music in the courtyard plaza.

The collections The majority of the museum's permanent collections are housed in the Ahmanson Building. Here magnificent examples of ancient Asian, Egyptian and pre-Columbian art, medieval and Renaissance paintings, works by 17th-century Dutch landscape specialists and 18th-century French Romantics have been gathered together with a feast of Impressionist, Fauvist, Cubist and Surrealist art. There is a dazzling array of British silver, diverse examples of European and American decorative arts, plus costumes and textiles, jewel-like Persian manuscripts and Ottoman ceramics. The museum's

The sculpture gardens (left) and the Japanese Pavilion (right) at LA County Museum of Art (LACMA)

collections of German 20th-century and Expressionist art are world class and the new Madina Collection of Islamic Art is significant.

Exhibitions and sculpture gardens In addition to housing selections from the permanent collections, the Anderson and Hammer buildings offer special display space, and LACMA is a great place to catch top-flight visiting exhibitions. The buildings are flanked by sculpture gardens with works by Rodin, Bourdelle, Calder and Alice Aycock.

Make a plan The museum complex is spread over five buildings. Its collections are so vast that there is far too much to be seen comfortably in a single visit, so it is advisable to plot a route around personal favorites with the aid of a layout plan (constantly changing) from the information booth.

THE BASICS

www.lacma.org
✚ H6
✉ 5905 Wilshire Boulevard, Midtown
☎ 323/857-6000
🕐 Mon, Tue, Thu 12–8, Fri 12–9, Sat–Sun 11–8. Closed Thanksgiving, Christmas
🍴 Plaza Café
🚌 20, 21, 22, 217
♿ Very good
💲 Moderate. Free every day after 5, unless an exhibit has a separate charge

Universal Studios Hollywood

HIGHLIGHTS

- Backdraft
- Back to The Future–The Ride
- Fear Factor Live
- Jurassic Park–The Ride
- Revenge of the Mummy–The Ride
- Shrek 4-D
- The Studio Tour
- Terminator 2: 3D
- Universal's House of Horrors
- WaterWorld show

TIPS

- Admission is free if you have a CityPass (▷ 30).
- A Front of Line Pass ($85) gets you priority boarding on all rides and reserved seating at all shows.

The world's biggest motion picture studio and theme park is a great day out. The renowned Studio Tour, Jurassic Park–The Ride and Terminator 2: 3D alone are worth the price of admission.

Back to the beginning Universal Studios' founder Carl Laemmle moved his movie studio facility to the Hollywood Hills in 1915 and inaugurated Universal Studios tours during the silent movie era. The arrival of the talkies put an end to live audiences until 1964, when trolley tours began; trolleys are still used to circle the 415-acre (168ha) backlot.

Orientation The Studio Tour, narrated by actress and comedienne Whoopi Goldberg, includes close encounters with old banana breath himself in

Universal Studios movie theme park offers an exciting day out for all the family

UNIVERSAL STUDIOS
HOLLYWOOD

THE BASICS

www.universalstudios
hollywood.com

🔰 H3

✉ 100 Universal City
Plaza (off I–101/Hollywood
Freeway)

☎ 818/622-3801;
800/UNIVERSAL

🕐 Summer 9–9, winter
10–6; longer hours at
weekends all year

🍴 Wide range of dining
and fast-food options

🚌 422, 423

Ⓜ Metro Red Line

♿ Good

💲 Very expensive;
children under 3 free

Kongfrontation; a chase sequence inspired by
The Fast and the Furious: Tokyo Drift; a simulated
flash flood introduced by weatherman Al Roker;
and classic locations from the *Psycho* house to
the Grinch's Whoville. Trolley tours depart from the
Upper Lot, which is also home to Revenge of the
Mummy–The Ride, Shrek 4-D, Nickelodeon Blast
Zone and half a dozen great shows and revues.

Take a ride A long escalator links the Upper Lot
to the Lower Lot, the heart of the working studio
complex. Here, Universal's Jurassic Park–The Ride
adventure visits a land of five-story dinosaurs built
with the help of aerospace scientists. There are
red-hot special effects at the Backdraft presentation, insight into behind-the-scenes technology at
the Special Effects Stages and audience bravery at
Fear Factor Live.

More to See

CAPITOL RECORDS TOWER
Welton Becket's 1954 tower houses the company that can list Sinatra and the Beach Boys among its signings, and is one of Hollywood's most famous landmarks. Though the architect denied it was intentional, it resembles a stack of records topped by a needle.

✚ J5 ✉ 1750 Vine Street, Hollywood 🚌 212, 217 Ⓜ Metro Red Line

EGYPTIAN THEATRE
This 1922 movie palace, home to Hollywood's first premiere (*Robin Hood* starring Douglas Fairbanks), has been restored to its original grandeur. Visitors can view *Forever Hollywood*, a film about Hollywood's celebrated, narrated by Sharon Stone.

✚ H5 ✉ 6712 Hollywood Boulevard ☎ 323/466-3456 ✋ Call for showtimes ✋ Moderate 🚌 212, 217 Ⓜ Metro Red Line

GREYSTONE PARK
The parklands surrounding oil millionaire Edward Doheny's 1928 Gothic mansion offer fine views over Beverly Hills (▷ 25).

✚ G5 ✉ 905 Loma Vista Drive, Beverly Hills ☎ 310/550-4654 🕐 Daily 10–5 (until 6 in summer) 🚌 2, 302 ✋ Free

HOLLYWOOD GUINNESS WORLD OF RECORDS MUSEUM
Trivia galore from The-Animal-with-the-Smallest-Brain-in-Proportion-to-Body-Size (a Stegosaurus) to the Most Biographed Female (Marilyn Monroe).

✚ H5 ✉ 6764 Hollywood Boulevard, Hollywood ☎ 323/463-6433 🕐 Sun–Thu 10–midnight, Fri–Sat 10–1am 🚌 212, 217 Ⓜ Metro Red Line ✋ Moderate

HOLLYWOOD HERITAGE MUSEUM
Cecil B. De Mille shot Hollywood's first full-length movie in this old horse barn in 1913. Moved from its site on Vine to the Paramount lot across from the Hollywood Bowl (▷ 44), it now houses film memorabilia and antique movie-making equipment.

✚ H4 ✉ 2100 N. Highland Avenue ☎ 323/874-2276 🕐 Sat–Sun 11–4 🚌 156, 426 ♿ Few ✋ Inexpensive

A statue outside the Capitol Records Tower

The Gothic mansion in Greystone Park

🅿 Heritage walking tour Sun 9am
(☎ 323/465-6716 for reservations)

HOLLYWOOD ROOSEVELT HOTEL

A romantic rendezvous for Clark Gable and his wife, where Errol Flynn supposedly invented his own gin cocktail behind the barber shop, and where David Niven slept in the servants' quarters before his star was born.
➕ H5 ✉ 7000 Hollywood Boulevard
☎ 323/466-7000 🕐 Daily 🚍 212, 217
Ⓜ Metro Red Line ♿ Few 💷 Free

LOS ANGELES ZOO

LA Zoo is filled with more than 1,200 animals from 350 species ranging from koalas to Komodo dragons, so there's plenty to see. In the mid-1990s the Zoo faced closure for its appalling conditions; since then, more "natural" habitats have been created, starting with the Chimps of Mahale Mountains reserve. The program is still ongoing, with the Campo Gorilla Reserve and Pachyderm Forest to be completed next.

➕ K3 ✉ 5333 Zoo Drive, Griffith Park
☎ 323/644-4200 🕐 Daily 10–5. Closed Christmas 🚍 96 ♿ Very good
💷 Moderate

MULHOLLAND DRIVE

This winding mountain road with terrific views runs from Hollywood west past Malibu (with an unpaved section through Topanga State Park). Access to the eastern section is off Laurel Canyon Boulevard; to the western section from Old Topanga Canyon Road.
➕ G4

MUSEUM OF TELEVISION AND RADIO

This tribute to more than 80 years of home entertainment investigates aspects of broadcasting from news to *Star Trek* make-up.
➕ F6 ✉ 465 N. Beverly Drive, Beverly Hills
☎ 310/786-1000 🕐 Wed–Sun 12–5
🚍 2, 4 ♿ Good 💷 Inexpensive

MUSEUM OF TOLERANCE

Opened in 1993, less than a year after the LA riots, the Museum of

Fantastic views from Mulholland Drive

Museum of Television and Radio

Tolerance focuses its attentions on both the dynamics of prejudice and racism in America, and the history of the Holocaust. High-tech interactive and experiential exhibits offer a challenging insight into the affects of bigotry. World War II artifacts and documents on the second floor provide the most moving memorial of all.

✚ F6 ✉ 9 Simon Wiesenthal Center, 9786 W. Pico Boulevard, West LA ☎ 310/553-8403 🕔 Apr–end Oct Mon–Thu 11–6.30, Fri 11–5, Sun 11–7.30 (Nov–Mar Fri until 3). Closed Jewish hols ♿ Very good ✋ Moderate ❓ Photo ID needed for admission

PETERSEN AUTOMOTIVE MUSEUM

Displaying more than the requisite classic cars, the Petersen Automotive Museum traces the automobile's evolution, along with celebrity cruisers and the physics behind motor cars and driving. This is the largest museum of its type in the US.

✚ H6 ✉ 6060 Wilshire Boulevard ☎ 323/930-2277 🕔 Tue–Sun 10–6. Closed major hols 🚌 20, 21, 22, 217 ♿ Very good ✋ Moderate

VIRGINIA ROBINSON MANSION AND GARDENS

The late society hostess Virginia Robinson's Mediterranean-style villa is set in 6.2 acres (2.5ha) of lush gardens and groves with palms, terraces and water features.

✚ F5 ✉ 1008 Elden Way, Beverly Hills ☎ 310/276-5367 🕔 Tue–Thu 10am and 1pm, Fri 10am (reservation only) 🚌 2, 302 ✋ Moderate

WARNER BROTHERS STUDIO VIP TOUR

A behind-the-scenes tour for the serious movie buff. Small groups (reservations advised; no children under 8) tour backlot sets, watch actual productions in progress where possible and learn about movie-making.

✚ H3 ✉ 4000 Warner Boulevard, Burbank ☎ 818/972-8687 🕔 Every half hour. Mon–Fri 8.30–4; extended hours in spring and summer 🚌 163 ♿ Few ✋ Very expensive

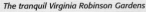

Go behind the scenes at the Warner Brothers Studio

The tranquil Virginia Robinson Gardens

Beverly Hills Loop

Stroll by unique architecture, expensive shops, lovely residences and a few swanky hotels.

DISTANCE: 2.2 miles (3.6km) **ALLOW:** 3–4 hours

START

BEVERLY WILSHIRE HOTEL
➕ F6 🚌 14, 21

1 Begin at the Beverly Wilshire Hotel (▷ 112) where Rodeo Drive meets Wilshire. The facade, famous long before its appearance in the film *Pretty Woman*, has housed a number of celebrity guests.

2 Cross Wilshire and meander through Via Rodeo. Continue up Rodeo Drive, taking note of the Anderton Court shops (332 N. Rodeo), which were designed by Frank Lloyd Wright.

3 Turn right on Brighton Way to Beverly Drive and left on Beverly Drive, to the Museum of Television and Radio (▷ 37) at the corner of Beverly Drive and Rodeo.

4 Continue north across Santa Monica Boulevard and turn left for one short block. Turn right on Rodeo and see the Gaudi-influenced O'Neill House (No. 507) just past the alley.

END

BEVERLY WILSHIRE HOTEL

8 Back on Wilshire, continue strolling east past the department stores—Nieman Marcus, Saks Fifth Avenue and Barneys (panel, ▷ 41) en route to the Beverly Wilshire.

7 Continue east on Wilshire and consider a stop at the luxurious Peninsula Beverly Hills hotel (▷ 112) for a pricey tea, offered every afternoon at 2.30 and 5. If you make this very short detour, you will turn right on S. Santa Monica.

6 Here is the Witch's House, which was built for a movie studio. Continue down Carmelita and turn left on Wilshire Boulevard. Walk east on Wilshire and notice the I. M. Pei-designed building at 2830 Wilshire.

5 Continue north. Turn left on Carmelita Avenue and proceed to the southwest corner of Carmelita and Walden.

Shopping

AARDVARKS
Barn-like vintage clothing store. Dinner jackets from bandleader-flash to butler's tails, frocks and feather boas, accessories and wig bin. Also in Pasadena and Venice.
H5 ✉ 7579 Melrose Avenue, West Hollywood
☎ 323/655-6769 🚍 10, 11

AMERICAN RAG
Vast secondhand clothes and accessories emporium. Tuxes, grunge, ex-military great coats, 1970s glam and 1980s unspeakable.
H6 ✉ 150 S. La Brea, Midtown ☎ 323/935-3154
🚍 14, 212

AMOEBA MUSIC
This Northern California independent music store has added a southern branch in Hollywood with the same stellar selection of new and used CDs and vinyl LPs. Occasional free performances.
J5 ✉ 6400 Sunset Boulevard ☎ 323/245-6400
🚍 2, 302

ANTIQUARIUS
A great place to browse: more than 30 shops specializing in antiques jewelry, silver, art glass and curios.
G5 ✉ 8840 Beverly Boulevard, West Hollywood
☎ 310/274-2363 🚍 14

BEVERLY CENTER
Major league mall with 150 upscale fashion, department and specialty stores, and cinemas and restaurants.
G6 ✉ 8500 Beverly Boulevard, West Hollywood
☎ 310/854-0071 🚍 14, 16, 218, 316

BODHI TREE
The New Age bookshop where Shirley MacLaine got metaphysical.
H5 ✉ 8585 Melrose Avenue, West Hollywood
☎ 310/659-1733 🚍 10, 11

BOOK SOUP
This voluminous bookstore has spawned a fashionable bistro next door. Classics to crime, reference books and more; the art history and movie sections are also good.
G5 ✉ 8818 Sunset Boulevard, West Hollywood
☎ 310/659-3110 🚍 2, 302, 429

A DIFFERENT LIGHT
A huge selection of gay and lesbian literature.

Evening readings.
G5 ✉ 8853 Santa Monica Boulevard, West Hollywood
☎ 310/854-6601 🚍 4, 304

FREDERICK'S OF HOLLYWOOD
Celebrated trashy-chic lingerie, brassieres that enhance "sans surgery," stiletto heels, feather boas—so kinky its cool.
H5 ✉ 6751 Hollywood Boulevard, Hollywood
☎ 323/957-5953 🚍 212, 217

FRED SEGAL
Legendary and eternally hip Melrose specialty store complex. Sportswear and designer collections for men, women and children; gifts, accessories, lingerie and luggage.
H5 ✉ 8100 Melrose Avenue, West Hollywood
☎ 323/651-4129 🚍 10, 11

GEMINI G.E.L.
Prints by top American/US-based 20th-century artists: Jasper Johns, Robert Rauschenberg, Richard Diebenkorn, David Hockney.
H5 ✉ 8365 Melrose Avenue, West Hollywood
☎ 323/651-0513 🚍 10, 11

THE GROVE AT FARMERS MARKET
Architectural styles range from Italian Renaissance to art deco at this huge complex.
H6 ✉ 3rd Street and Fairfax Avenue, Midtown
🚍 141, 217

HOLLYWOOD AND HIGHLAND

Five-floor open-air retail and entertainment complex, with chain establishments, boutiques, eateries, cinemas and the Kodak Theatre.

✚ H5 ✉ Hollywood Boulevard and Highland Avenue ☎ 323/467-6412 🚌 212, 217

HOLLYWOOD BOULEVARD

In the myriad souvenir shops you'll find everything from T-shirts to coffee mugs, all emblazoned with some tribute to Hollywood and the movies.

✚ J5 ✉ Hollywood Boulevard Ⓜ Metro Red Line 🚌 212, 217

IT'S A WRAP

Movie and television studio wardrobe departments offload their extravagances at this bulging Valley shop. Second location at 1164 S. Robertson Boulevard.

✚ H2 ✉ 3315 W. Magnolia Boulevard, Burbank ☎ 818/567-7366 🚌 183

JAY WOLF

Tucked away in a small courtyard, Wolf specializes in discreet and comfortable modern designer clothing (Paul Smith, Hugo Boss) for men and women.

✚ G6 ✉ 517 N. Robertson Boulevard, West Hollywood ☎ 310/273-9893 🚌 10, 11, 220

LA EYEWORKS

From the town that never removes its shades, face furniture for every occasion.

✚ H5 ✉ 7407 Melrose Avenue, West Hollywood ☎ 323/653-8255 🚌 10, 11

LARRY EDMUNDS' BOOKSHOP

A small but rich trawling ground for cinematic bibliophiles, stocking all sorts of film and theater-related tomes, plus posters and stills.

✚ H5 ✉ 6644 Hollywood Boulevard, Hollywood ☎ 323/463-3273 🚌 212, 217

LISA KLINE

For more than a decade, the Robertson branch has been the place to go for the latest fashions and for pieces from up-and-coming designers. This new

DEPARTMENT STORES

As if Rodeo Drive were not enough to keep Beverly Hills' gold card-toting matrons occupied between lunches, LA's "Department Store Row" lies a mere stretch-limo's length away. Neiman Marcus (✉ 9700 Wilshire Boulevard ☎ 310/550-5900), Saks Fifth Avenue (✉ 9600 Wilshire Boulevard ☎ 310/275-4211), and Barneys New York (✉ 9570 Wilshire Boulevard ☎ 310/276-4400) offer the full complement of fashions, furnishings, gifts and cosmetics.

Beverly Hills branch also carries fashion-forward clothes and accessories.

✚ F6 ✉ 315 S. Beverly Drive ☎ 310/691-1070 🚌 220

LOUIS STERN FINE ARTS

Well-respected gallery renowned for Latin-American, Impressionist, 20th-century and contemporary work.

✚ H5 ✉ 9002 Melrose Avenue, West Hollywood ☎ 310/276-0147 🚌 10, 11

MARGO LEAVIN GALLERY

Photography, paintings, sculpture and works on paper at this cutting-edge contemporary art gallery.

✚ G6 ✉ 812 N. Robertson Boulevard, West Hollywood ☎ 310/273-0603 🚌 4, 220

MAXFIELD'S

Designer fashions for men and women, plus lovely furniture, antiques, jewelry and housewares.

✚ H5 ✉ 8825 Melrose Avenue, West Hollywood ☎ 310/274-8800 🚌 10, 11, 220

MELROSE AVENUE

A 3-mile (5km) strip of the esoteric and exotic from cutting-edge fashion and retro boutiques to galleries and gift shops. Riveting window-shopping, dining and people-watching.

✚ H5 ✉ Melrose Avenue (between Highland Avenue and Doheny Drive), Hollywood 🚌 10, 11

PLASTICA
Woven bags, chopsticks, teapots, sandals, potato mashers and more—all made from plastic.
➕ H6 ✉ 8405 W. 3rd Street ☎ 323/655-1051 🚌 16, 218

PRADA
One of the trendiest stores in the city, offering hip clothes (at a high price). For those seeking the approval of the LA fashion police.
➕ F6 ✉ 343 N. Rodeo Drive, Beverly Hills
☎ 310/278-8661 🚌 2, 14, 27

RODEO DRIVE
LA's answer to London's Bond Street and Rome's Via Condotti, Rodeo Drive is a gold-plated shopping experience. There are enough top designer clothes and accessories boutiques and chic malls here to send most credit cards into meltdown.
➕ F6 ✉ Rodeo Drive (between Santa Monica and Wilshire boulevards), Beverly Hills 🚌 4, 20, 21, 22

SAMUEL FRENCH THEATER & FILM BOOKSHOP
For true aficionados and wannabe movie writers, this is the place to pick up specialist books and essential and obscure film and theater scripts. Knowledgeable staff.
➕ H5 ✉ 7623 Sunset Boulevard, West Hollywood
☎ 323/876-0570 🚌 2

SOOLIP PAPERIE & PRESS
Amazing stationery shop: racks of colorful hand-made papers, colored inks, hip pens and desk accessories. Check out the Bungalow across the garden courtyard for its delectable range of silk pyjamas, sumptuous bed covers and alluring bath products.
➕ H5 ✉ 8646 Melrose Avenue, West Hollywood
☎ 310/360-0545 🚌 10, 11

SUNSET PLAZA
An exclusive little cluster of ultrafashionable boutiques and sidewalk bistros on "The Strip."
➕ G5 ✉ Sunset Boulevard (between San Vicente and La

DESIGN DISTRICT
The interior design capital of the Pacific Rim, West Hollywood has a wealth of art and antiques galleries, plus around 300 design stores and showrooms main-ly around the west end of Melrose Avenue and San Vicente Boulevard. Here is the Pacific Design Center (aka "The Blue Whale" for its size and color), which harbors more than 200 showrooms offering furniture, fabrics, lighting and kitchen products. They are open to the general public (Mon–Fri 9–5), though some may require an appointment.

Cienega boulevards), West Hollywood 🚌 2

UNIVERSAL CITYWALK
Eclectic gifts, souvenirs and entertainment outside Universal Studios Hollywood.
➕ H3 ✉ 1000 Universal Center Drive, Universal City
☎ 818/622-4455 🚌 422

WACKO
Part shop, part gallery, with items for every (albeit wacky) taste and pocket.
➕ K5 ✉ 4633 Hollywood Boulevard, Hollywood
☎ 323/663-0122 🚌 26, 217

WANNA BUY A WATCH?
Vintage and contem-porary timepieces from Bulova to Betty Boop, Tiffany dress watches, US military issue, plus antique diamond and art deco jewelry.
➕ H5 ✉ 8465 Melrose Avenue, West Hollywood
☎ 323/653-0467 🚌 10, 11

WASTELAND
Come to Melrose, of course, for vintage clothes for men and women. Last year's designer labels share spaces with '70s gear, plus shoes, leather and suede.
➕ H5 ✉ 7428 Melrose Avenue, West Hollywood
☎ 323/653-3028 🚌 10

Entertainment and Nightlife

ARENA
Huge dance club in a former warehouse, with theme nights from house and hip-hop to Latino. Live bands and DJs (Thu–Sun), gay and lesbian night (Tue).
✚ H5 ✉ 6655 Santa Monica Boulevard, Hollywood
☎ 323/462-0714 🚌 4, 304

AVALON HOLLYWOOD
Formerly the Palace, this renovated club is now sleek and minimalist, with a restaurant and a smaller more elite club inside called the Spider.
✚ J5 ✉ 1735 N. Vine Street, Hollywood ☎ 323/467-4571
Ⓜ Metro Red Line
🚌 212, 217

THE BAKED POTATO
One of LA's best contemporary jazz spots. The stuffed baked potatoes aren't bad either.
✚ H4 ✉ 3787 Cahuenga Boulevard (at Lankershim), Studio City ☎ 818/980-1615
Ⓜ Metro Red Line
🚌 422, 423

BARNEY'S BEANERY
Convivial bar with pool tables and a Tex-Mex dining room.
✚ G5 ✉ 8447 Santa Monica Boulevard, West Hollywood ☎ 323/654-2287 🚌 4

B. B. KING'S BLUES CLUB
Restaurant and club serving Delta-style food and live blues, occasionally from the master himself.

Gospel brunch on Sunday.
✚ H3 ✉ Universal City Walk, Universal City
☎ 818/622-5464 Ⓜ Metro Red Line 🚌 422, 433

BLUE ON BLUE AT THE AVALON HOTEL
Southern California, just as you want it to be: poolside cocktails in an intimate setting. Specialty drinks include a pomegranate mojito.
✚ F6 ✉ 9400 W. Olympic Boulevard, Beverly Hills
☎ 310/277-5221 🚌 7, 28

BOB'S BIG BOY
Serried ranks of LA's coolest customized hot rods wheel up at this Valley diner on a Friday night.
✚ H3 ✉ 4211 Riverside Drive, Burbank ☎ 818/843-9334

CAT "N" FIDDLE PUB
Young crowd comes to enjoy the outdoor patio, English beer on tap and visiting rock musicians.
✚ H5 ✉ 6530 Sunset Boulevard, Hollywood
☎ 323/468-3800 🚌 2

OPENING TIMES
Most music bars are open nightly from around 9pm until 2am. Headline acts tend to go on after 11pm, when the clubs start to liven up. Clubs and music bars are often closed on Sunday and Monday nights. Call ahead.

COMEDY STORE
Three stages showcase funsters who are up-and-coming, have made it, or are just plain HUGE. One of the city's premier clubs.
✚ G5 ✉ 8433 Sunset Boulevard, West Hollywood
☎ 323/656-6225 🚌 2

THE DERBY
Swanky and glamorous, where locals dress up and come out to swing-dance the night away.
✚ K4 ✉ 4500 Los Feliz Boulevard, Los Feliz/Silverlake
☎ 323/663-8979
🚌 180, 181

FLORENTINE GARDENS
A dressy young clientele frequents this hip dance-teria (Sat) with cool DJs and free buffet.
✚ H5 ✉ 5955 Hollywood Boulevard, Hollywood
☎ 323/464-0706 Ⓜ Metro Red Line 🚌 212, 217

FOUR SEASONS
Celebrity-watching in a refined, relaxed hotel lounge setting.
✚ G6 ✉ 300 S. Doheny Drive, Beverly Hills
☎ 310/273-2222 🚌 4, 27, 304

GRIFFITH PARK GOLF
Two 18-hole and two 9-hole courses. Facilities include club rental, carts, proshop, dining and night-lit driving range.
✚ J3 ✉ Griffith Park Drive, Griffith Park ☎ Information and reservations: 323/663-2555 🚌 96

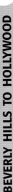
GRIFFITH PARK TENNIS
More than two dozen courts (available both day and night) at three locations. Reservations required. Drop-bys accepted space permitting.
🚻 J3 ✉ Griffith Park Drive and Vermont Canyon, Griffith Park ☎ Information and reservations: 323/664-3521, 323/661-5318 🚌 96

GROUNDLINGS THEATER
Talented improvizational comedy troupe in short-run shows. Very popular—reservations are necessary.
🚻 H5 ✉ 7307 Melrose Avenue, West Hollywood ☎ 323/934-9700 🚌 10, 11

HOLLYWOOD BOWL
Much-loved outdoor venue for the Los Angeles Philharmonic Orchestra's Symphony Under the Stars series (Jun–Sep) and other performances.
🚻 H4 ✉ 2301 N. Highland Avenue, Hollywood ☎ 323/850-2000 🚌 426

HOUSE OF BLUES
This tin-shack theme restaurant on Sunset attracts massive crowds and a generous sprinkling of celebs for Southern food and headline blues-rock acts.
🚻 G5 ✉ 8430 Sunset Boulevard, West Hollywood ☎ 323/848-5100 🚇 Metro Red Line 🚌 2

HYDE LOUNGE
This teeny Hollywood hotspot has a DJ, a small plates bar menu, and plenty of stargazing (think the Hilton sisters and Lindsay Lohan). Admittance by guest list only.
🚻 G5 ✉ 8029 W. Sunset Boulevard, Hollywood ☎ 323/656-4933 🚌 2, 217

THE IMPROV
A popular new-material testing ground for big-name comics. Best to reserve a table.
🚻 H5 ✉ 8162 Melrose Avenue, West Hollywood ☎ 323/651-2583 🚌 10, 11

LUCKY STRIKES LANE
Video screens, DJs and lots of neon add flash to this 12-lane bowling alley in the Hollywood and Highland complex. After 7pm, guests must be at least 21.
🚻 H5 ✉ 6801 Hollywood Boulevard, Suite 143 ☎ 323/467-7776 🚇 Metro Red Line 🚌 212, 217

THE MINT
Long-standing small blues

CLUB CIRCUIT
For the dedicated clubber with plenty of stamina and deep pockets, LA NightHawks (☎ 310/392-1500) can arrange a VIP night on the town. Door-to-door limousines and no-hassle entry to a host of music, cabaret, dance and comedy clubs for a fun night out.

bar with a faithful following and great music and atmosphere. Live jazz on Monday night.
🚻 G6 ✉ 6010 W. Pico Boulevard, Midtown ☎ 323/954-9400 🚌 SM5, 7, 12, 13

MOLLY MALONE'S IRISH PUB
Venerable Irish-American institution. Guinness, darts and Irish music.
🚻 H5 ✉ 575 S. Fairfax Avenue (south of Melrose Avenue), Midtown ☎ 323/935-1577 🚌 10, 11, 217

MUSSO & FRANK
Hollywood's oldest and most celebrated bar/grill.
🚻 H5 ✉ 6667 Hollywood Boulevard, Hollywood ☎ 323/467-7788 🚇 Metro Red Line 🚌 212, 217

PEARL
This supper club plays host to sensuous cabaret, Karaoke From Hell (Tue), with a live band providing the music, and plenty of celeb sightings. Dinner menu is Asian influenced.
🚻 G5 ✉ 665 N. Robertson Boulevard, West Hollywood ☎ 310/358-9191 🚌 16, 220

RAGE
Packed West Hollywood gay club for boys, serving Top 40, house, Latin and progressive, drag comedy and variety.
🚻 G5 ✉ 8911 Santa Monica Boulevard, West Hollywood ☎ 310/652-7055 🚌 4, 304

THE ROXY
Small, steamy rock venue, showcasing major recording acts and new bands via a sound system that will knock your socks off.
🚩 G5 ✉ 9009 Sunset Boulevard, West Hollywood ☎ 310/276-2222 or 310/278-9457 🚃 2

SAMUEL OSCHIN PLANETARIUM
Cross the universe in this 300-seat theater, with its fancy new projection and sound systems. Tickets sold day of show only.
🚩 J4 ✉ 2800 E. Observatory Road ☎ 213/473-0800 ⏰ Shows approximately hourly Tue–Fri 12.45–8.45; Sat–Sun 10.45–8.45 🚃 96

SILENT MOVIE THEATER
It's fitting that the USA's last operational silent movie theater—renovated in 1999—is in this town. Organists offer musical accompaniment for each screening, and filmgoers can relax in the cappuccino lounge.
🚩 H5 ✉ 611 N. Fairfax Avenue ☎ 323/655-2520 🚃 10, 217

SKY BAR
Glamorous Mondrian Hotel (▷ 112) poolside bar with fantastic city views. Open only to hotel guests and those with reservations.
🚩 G5 ✉ 8440 Sunset Boulevard, West Hollywood ☎ 323/650-8999 🚃 2

THE STANDARD
A super-groovy venue where hipsters gather for cocktails amid shag-pile carpeting and bubble chairs.
🚩 G5 ✉ 8300 Sunset Boulevard, West Hollywood ☎ 323/650-9090 🚃 2

THIBIANT EUROPEAN DAY SPA
A roll-call of Hollywood's most glamorous female movie stars come here for massages, facials, manicures, make-up and skin treatments.
🚩 F6 ✉ 449 N. Cañon Drive, Beverly Hills ☎ 310/278-7565 🚃 2, 14, 576

THE HIGH LIFE

Can't afford $350 a night for a swank hotel? Consider a martini at a hotel bar instead. Views and people-watching perks don't cost extra. In addition to Sky Bar (▷ this page) and Four Seasons (▷ 43), try one of the following: the Beverly Wilshire (▷ 112) ✉ 9500 Wilshire Boulevard ☎ 310/275-5200) Sunset Tower Hotel (✉ 8358 Sunset Boulevard ☎ 323/654-7100) Sunset Marquis' Bar 1200 (✉ 1200 N. Alta Loma Road ☎ 310/657-1333) Peninsula Hotel Bar (✉ 9882 Little Santa Monica Boulevard ☎ 310/551-2888).

THE TROUBADOUR
Doug Weston's venerable venue has staged live premier-league rock and folk music acts since the 1960s.
🚩 G5 ✉ 9081 Santa Monica Boulevard, West Hollywood ☎ 310/276-6168 🚃 4, 304

THE VIPER ROOM
Co-owned by Johnny Depp, the Viper draws cool crowds and big names. There are jam and dance nights.
🚩 G5 ✉ 8852 Sunset Boulevard, West Hollywood ☎ 310/358-1880 🚃 2

WHISKY A GO GO
Though there is less "Go-Go" these days, this Sunset Strip stalwart continues to be a haven for hard rockers.
🚩 G5 ✉ 8901 Sunset Boulevard, West Hollywood ☎ 310/652-4202 🚃 2

WINSTON'S
There's no sign and no velvet ropes outside, but you still might spy a celeb inside. DJs spin nightly.
🚩 H5 ✉ 7746 Santa Monica Boulevard, West Hollywood ☎ 323/654-0105 🚃 4, 304

Restaurants

PRICES

Prices are approximate, based on a 3-course meal for one person.

$$$$ over $50
$$$ $30–$50
$$ $15–$30
$ under $15

BARNEY GREENGRASS ($)

The smoked fish, including sturgeon, salmon and cod, is renowned at this chic room atop Barneys New York department store.
➕ F6 ✉ 9570 Wilshire Boulevard, Beverly Hills ☎ 310/777-5877 🕐 Breakfast, lunch daily 🚌 20, 21, 720

THE BELVEDERE ($$$)

The dining room at the Peninsula (▷ 112) is noted for its "small bites." These allow you to sample the chef's signature dishes. Exquisite presentation, impeccable service and a celebrity clientele.
➕ F6 ✉ 9882 Little Santa Monica Boulevard ☎ 310/788-2306 🕐 Breakfast, lunch, dinner daily 🚌 21, 27, 316

LA BREA BAKERY ($)

Although this bakery is attached to a terrific Italian restaurant (Campanile), the thing to go for is brunch.
➕ H6 ✉ 624 S. La Brea Avenue 🕐 Brunch Sat–Sun, lunch daily ☎ 323/939-6813 🚌 212

BRIGHTON COFFEE SHOP ($)

An authentic 1930s coffee shop serving sandwich favorites such as grilled cheese, meat loaf and tuna.
➕ F6 ✉ 9600 Brighton Way, Beverly Hills ☎ 310/276-7732 🕐 Breakfast, lunch daily 🚌 20, 21, 720

CANTER'S ($)

Classic Fairfax District deli serving kosher specials, huge pastrami sandwiches, homemade pickles and waitress banter 24 hours a day.
➕ H5 ✉ 419 N. Fairfax Avenue, Midtown ☎ 323/651-2030 🚌 14, 217

CHAYA ($$$)

Minimalist with a Japanese sensibility that's also evident in the innovative and intriguing

CALIFORNIA CUISINE

Fresh, seasonal, inventive and health-conscious: These words define California cuisine, the cooking style launched in 1971 by celebrity chef Alice Waters in her lauded Berkeley restaurant, Chez Panisse. The approach caught on throughout the state, with chefs learning to take advantage of seasonal ingredients and appreciate nature's bounty. A fall menu, for example, might include a salad tossed with nuts, butternut squash soup and pumpkin risotto.

East-meets-West menu. Second location in Venice.
➕ G6 ✉ 8741 Alden Drive, Beverly Hills ☎ 310/859-8833 🕐 Lunch, dinner daily 🚌 14, 16

CHIN CHIN ($)

Healthful Chinese LA chain famous for its Chinese chicken salad, low-fat alternatives and chocolate-covered fortune cookies. Other outposts in Beverly Hills, Brentwood, Marina del Rey and Studio City.
➕ G5 ✉ 8618 Sunset Boulevard, West Hollywood ☎ 310/652-1818 🕐 Lunch, dinner daily 🚌 2

EL CHOLO ($$)

LA institution (est. 1927) serving Mexican fare in hacienda-style surroundings with patio tables. Another outpost in Santa Monica.
➕ J6 ✉ 1121 S. Western Avenue, Midtown ☎ 323/734-2773 🚌 207, 357

CRUSTACEAN ($$$)

Fabulous 1930s Indochina-style interior where a star-studded clientele feast on Vietnamese/French fare, including a "secret" menu of family recipes.
➕ F6 ✉ 9646 S. Santa Monica Boulevard, Beverly Hills ☎ 310/205-8990 ✉ Mon–Sat 12–7.30 🚌 14, 27

DOUGHBOYS ($–$$)

Tempting sandwiches, pizzas, homemade soups,

and a tantalizing array of breads and baked goods make this a busy destination for any meal of the day.

➕ G6 ✉ 8136 W. 3rd Street ☎ 323/651-4202 🕐 Daily 7am to midnight 🚌 16, 217

ELECTRIC LOTUS ($)
Hidden in a corner mini-mall, this Indian eatery delights with its surprisingly exotic decor, and excellent curries.

➕ K4 ✉ 4656 Franklin Avenue, Los Feliz ☎ 323/953-0040 🕐 Lunch, dinner daily 🚌 26

GREENBLATT'S ($)
A haven for homesick New Yorkers, with deli favorites from cheesecake to corned beef.

➕ G5 ✉ 8017 Sunset Boulevard, West Hollywood ☎ 323/656-0606 🕐 Breakfast, lunch, dinner daily 🚌 2

THE IVY ($$$)
Reservations are a must for this film-folk hangout. Try the white-chocolate lemon and walnut cake. Terrace dining.

➕ G6 ✉ 113 N. Robertson Boulevard, Beverly Hills ☎ 310/274-8303 🕐 Lunch, dinner daily 🚌 14, 16, 20, 21, 105

KOKOMO ($)
Freshly baked muffins, deli sandwiches, steaming bowls of tasty gumbo, salads—all good reasons to brave the busy Farmers Market.

➕ H6 ✉ Farmers Market, 6333 W. 3rd Street, Midtown ☎ 323/933-0773 🕐 Breakfast, lunch, dinner daily 🚌 14, 217

LAWRY'S THE PRIME RIB ($$$)
Aged prime rib, Yorkshire pudding, creamed spinach and horseradish sauce. Club-style surroundings; established in 1938.

➕ G6 ✉ 100 N. La Cienega Boulevard, Beverly Hills ☎ 310/652-2827 🕐 Dinner daily 🚌 20, 21, 105

LOCANDA VENETA ($$$)
Simple northern Italian cuisine in a robust, lively setting. Try a booth.

➕ H6 ✉ 8638 W. 3rd Street ☎ 310/274-1893 🕐 Lunch Mon–Fri, dinner daily 🚌 16, 217

MIDNIGHT MEALS
Restaurants in LA are not typically open late, but you can find a meal at midnight and into the wee hours. For cheap eats, Pink's Famous Chili Dogs (▷ 48) is open till 2am (until 3am on weekends) and Canter's (▷ 46), a deli on Fairfax, never closes. A bit more upscale is Kate Mantilini (✉ 9101 Wilshire Blvd. ☎ 310/278-3699), which serves American comfort food to an industry crowd until midnight or 1am (until 2am on weekends).

LUCQUES ($$$$)
Excellent California cuisine in a warm, inviting atmosphere. Sunday suppers are a good deal: $40 for a three-course fixed menu.

➕ G5 ✉ 8474 Melrose Avenue ☎ 323/655-6277 🕐 Lunch Tue–Sat, dinner daily 🚌 10, 11

LUNA PARK ($$)
A popular San Francisco restaurant also pleases LA diners with old-fashioned comfort food like breaded pork cutlets, baby back ribs and s'mores for dessert.

➕ H6 ✉ 672 S. La Brea Avenue ☎ 323/934-2110 🕐 Lunch, dinner daily 🚌 20, 21, 212

MEXICO CITY ($)
Los Feliz locals approve of the retro decor, superb enchiladas, Yucatan-style pork and mouthwatering shrimp dishes.

➕ K4 ✉ 2121 Hillhurst Avenue, Los Feliz ☎ 323/661-7227 🕐 Lunch Wed–Sun, dinner daily 🚌 26

MORTON'S ($$$$)
Stylish film-industry favorite packed with celebs grazing from the American menu.

➕ H5 ✉ 8764 Melrose Avenue, West Hollywood ☎ 310/276-5205 🕐 Lunch, dinner Mon–Fri; dinner Sat 🚌 10, 11

MR. CHOW ($$$$)
Agents and producers have spent more than 30

years having power lunches at this legendary Chinese restaurant.
➕ F6 ✉ 344 N. Camden Drive, Beverly Hills ☎ 310/278-9911 🕐 Lunch Mon–Fri, dinner daily 🚌 20, 21, 720

MUSSO & FRANK GRILL ($$)
Legendary Hollywood restaurant with film-noir flavor, traditional American dishes and perfectly mixed cocktails.
➕ H5 ✉ 6667 Hollywood Boulevard, Hollywood ☎ 323/467-5123 🕐 Lunch, dinner Tue–Sat 🚌 212, 217

NEWSROOM CAFÉ ($)
Excellent people-watching along with healthy salads, smoothies and good vegetarian selections.
➕ G6 ✉ 120 N. Robertson Boulevard ☎ 310/652-4444 🕐 Breakfast, lunch, dinner daily 🚌 20, 720, SM2

OFF VINE ($$–$$$)
Housed in an early 20th-century Craftsman-style bungalow, this restaurant serves American fare indoors by the roaring fire or outdoors on the bougainvillea-scented porch.
➕ J5 ✉ 6263 Leland Way, Hollywood ☎ 323/962-1900 🕐 Lunch, dinner daily 🚌 2, 212

ORTOLAN ($$$$)
One of LA's top chefs serves French food in an elegant but informal setting at his top-flight restaurant. Actress Jeri Ryan is also a partner.

➕ G6 ✉ 8338 W. 3rd Street, Los Angeles ☎ 323/653-3300 🕐 Dinner Tue–Sat 🚌 16

PALM RESTAURANT ($$$)
Noisy, no-nonsense, highly rated New York-style steak house, renowned for thick cuts of meat and enormous lobsters.
➕ G5 ✉ 9001 Santa Monica Boulevard, West Hollywood ☎ 310/550-8811 🕐 Mon–Fri lunch; dinner daily 🚌 4

PINK'S FAMOUS CHILI DOGS ($)
This takeout stand serves foot-long jalepeño dogs, burgers and tamales until 2am (3am Fri and Sat).
➕ H5 ✉ 709 N. La Brea ☎ 323/931-4223 🚌 212

HOTEL DINING
Diners will discover that top hotels house many of the city's finest restaurants. The Hotel Bel-Air Restaurant (▷ 112) serves California-French cuisine and wins raves for decor and service; the romantic Belvedere in the Peninsula Beverly Hills (▷ 46, 112) showcases American fare, including a sophisticated macaroni and cheese; and the Beverly Wilshire hotel (▷ 112) houses Cut, the Wolfgang Puck steak house designed by architect Richard Meier, more famous for designing the Getty Center (▷ 70).

SONORA CAFÉ ($$$)
Sophisticated Southwestern cuisine and home-on-the-range decor.
➕ H6 ✉ 180 S. La Brea Avenue, Midtown ☎ 323/857-1800 🕐 Lunch Tue–Fri, dinner Tue–Sun 🚌 14

SPAGO BEVERLY HILLS ($$$$)
The Beverly Hills outpost of Wolfgang Puck's legendary chain remains the premier place to rub elbows with the rich and famous.
➕ F6 ✉ 176 N. Canon Drive ☎ 310/385-0880 🕐 Lunch Mon–Sat, dinner daily 🚌 2, 14, 20, 21

EL TORITO GRILL ($$)
Busy, fun place serving a wide range of Mexican and Southwestern dishes.
➕ F6 ✉ 9595 Wilshire Boulevard, Beverly Hills ☎ 310/550-1599 🕐 Lunch, dinner daily 🚌 20, 21, 22

TRADER VIC'S ($$$)
This long-beloved favorite turns out Polynesian food and tropical cocktails.
➕ F6 ✉ 9876 Wilshire Boulevard, Beverly Hills ☎ 310/276-6345 🕐 Dinner daily 🚌 20, 21, 720

VILLAGE COFFEE SHOP ($)
Laid-back, friendly haunt of creative types in the Hollywood Hills; good home-cooked food.
➕ J4 ✉ 2695 N. Beachwood Drive, Hollywood ☎ 323/467-5398 🕐 Breakfast, lunch daily 🚌 208

Downtown LA has been revitalized by the construction of buildings like the Walt Disney Concert Hall and the cathedral, and by the influx of new residents buying condos and lofts.

LOS
ANGELE

NORTH ALVARADO STREET

We

5

6

MacArthur
Park

West 3rd Street

WILSHIRE BOULEVARD

West Olympic Boulevard

South Alvarado Street

Richard J Riorda
Central Librar

West Pico Boulevard

Gra
Hope F

Venice Boulevard

West Washington Boulevard

7

South Normandie Avenue

South Vermont Avenue

South Hoover Street

South Figueroa Street

South

South

Broad

East Adams Boulev

HARBOR FREEWAY

West Jefferson Boulevard

Main Street

West 36th Place

University
of Southern
California

East

East Jefferson Boulevar

Exposition Boulevard

California
Science
Center

Natural History
Museum of LA County

Exposition
Park

African-American
Museum

Rose Garden

West Martin Luther King Jr Boulevard

East Martin Luther King Jr Boulev

Wilson
Field

Avalon Boulevard

8

Theresa
Lindsay Park

West Vernon Avenue

South Figueroa Street

East Vernon Avenue

0   1 km

0   1 mile

9

H   J   K

West Sunset Boulevard

PASADENA FREEWAY

Temple Street

North Broadway

North Main Street

**Cathedral
of Our
Lady of
the Angels**

**El Pueblo de
Los Angeles**

**MOCA at
California
Plaza**

Grand

Walt Disney
Concert Hall
St.

Union Station

**Bradbury
Building**

City Hall

North Spring

**MOCA at the
Geffen Contemporary**

**Grand
Central
Market**

**Little
Tokyo**

**Japanese American
National Museum**

**Angels
Flight
Railway**

Avenue

East 4th Street

EAST 6TH STREET

Street

**BROADWAY
HISTORIC
THEATER DISTRICT**

East 9th Street

Alameda

SANTA

East

South

East Olympic Boulevard

MONICA

FREEWAY

Washington Boulevard

South Alameda Street

Ⓛ   Ⓜ   Ⓝ

Grand Central Market

Sawdust coats the floor and butchers' knives chop-chop and thud away on a dozen counters, just as they have since 1917 at this bustling, thriving Downtown LA landmark.

Downtown's historic larder LA's largest and oldest food market, a maze of closely packed stalls, first opened its doors in 1917, and the hangar-like building has been feeding the Downtown district ever since. In those days, Broadway was LA's poshest thoroughfare, while today it is the heart of the city's crowded Hispanic shopping district. The market goes from busy to heaving on Saturday, when the noise and the bustle is unbelievable.

Chilies and cacti For anyone who loves food or markets, Grand Central is a real find. A fantastic

Fresh produce and inexpensive take-out stands are the order of the day at Grand Central Market

feast for the eyes, it is also a great place to grab picnic food or stop for a snack. Chili peppers, avocados and big beef tomatoes are stacked into glossy piles alongside stalks of celery, potatoes in myriad hues, huge bunches of bananas and pyramids of oranges, lemons and apples. Among the less familiar offerings are prickly pears, cactus leaves and dozens of different types of fresh and dried chilies in varying degrees of ferocity. The Mexican butchers display bits of beasts you would rather not even think about. There are more than 50 stalls in all, including fish merchants and tortilla makers, confectioners, delicatessens selling cheese and cold meats, spice merchants, dried fruit and nut sellers and the Chinese herbal medicine man. Take-out food stands do a roaring trade in Mexican snacks, and there are quick-bite stops with tables and chairs near the Hill Street exit.

THE BASICS

www.grandcentralsquare.
com

✚ L6

✉ 317 S. Broadway

☎ 213/624-2378

🕐 Daily 9–6

🍴 Several Mexican fast-food take-out stands, Chinese noodle café, deli, bakery and a juice bar

Ⓢ Civic Center

🚌 DASH D

🚋 Angels Flight

♿ None

💲 Free

Little Tokyo

HIGHLIGHTS

● The annual cherry blossom festival in April
● A performance by the East West Players
● The Go for Broke Monument, which commemorates nearly 16,000 Japanese-American World War II veterans

TIP

● Check www.jaccc.org for information about upcoming events and performances.

The hub of LA's Japanese-American community is pleasantly low-key and walkable. You'll find surprise outposts of Japanese landscaping tucked into the concrete jungle.

Historical notes Bounded by 1st and 3rd, Los Angeles and Alameda streets, this area was first settled at the end of the 19th century. Several historic buildings remain on 1st Street, which leads to the Japanese American National Museum (▷ 61).

Sushi and *shiatsu* Over the road, among the neat green pompoms of pollarded trees and bright blue tile roofs, Japanese Village Plaza's 40 restaurants and small shops, exotic supermarkets, sushi bars and *shiatsu* massage parlors make for interesting browsing. You can then cross 2nd Street for

Find temples, landscaped gardens and Japanese restaurants among the skyscrapers of Little Tokyo

the Japanese-American Cultural and Community Center, where the Doizaki Gallery exhibits Japanese artworks. The adjacent Japan America Theater presents contemporary and traditional Japanese performances such as Noh and Kabuki theater productions. Outside, a 1,000ft (304m) installation commemorates a timeline spanning six decades of Japanese-American history.

Garden oasis Another feature of the plaza is the delightful James Irvine Garden, a Japanese-style oasis encircled by a stream, with paths, bridges, stepping stones, trees and flowering shrubs such as azaleas. There is more elegant Japanese landscaping nearby, outside the Higashi Hongwanji Buddhist Temple at No. 505 E. 3rd Street, where dwarf pines, grassy tuffets and rock arrangements front the graceful neo-traditional facade.

THE BASICS

www.visitlittletokyo.com

➕ L6

🚌 DASH A

Japanese-American Cultural and Community Center

www. jaccc.org

✉ Noguchi Plaza, 244 S. San Pedro Street, Suite 505

☎ 213/628-2725. Japan America Theater: 213/680-3700; Doizaki Gallery: 213/628-2725

Museum of Contemporary Art

TOP **25**

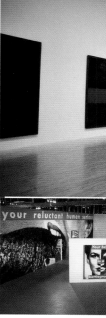

HIGHLIGHTS

Works by:
- De Kooning
- Giacometti
- Mondrian
- Pollock
- Oldenburg
- Hockney

TIPS

- The entry ticket gains you admission to both main museums, and there is a free shuttle bus service between them.
- Celebrity chef Joachim Splichal created the menu at Patinette.

A single museum with two addresses a mile (1.6km) apart, and a third across town, MOCA has a growing catalogue of post-1940 artworks that constitutes one of the most important contemporary art collections in the US.

Downtown From the outside, MOCA at California Plaza, designed by Japanese architect Arata Isozaki, is a construct of geometric cubes and pyramids clad in red brick, while the inside is all blond wood and vast white spaces—a fitting environment for the pieces on display. MOCA's downtown gallery presents a frequently changing schedule of both shows drawn from the extensive permanent collection and touring exhibitions. The busy calendar also introduces newly commissioned projects and works by established and emerging artists in a

The Museum of Contemporary Art consists of three galleries: the main Arata Isozaki-designed MOCA building, Geffen Contemporary and a satellite gallery in the Pacific Design Center

broad variety of media. The emphasis may be on temporary exhibitions, but there is also a strong permanent collection, with works by de Kooning, Lichtenstein, Arbus, Rothko and Warhol, among others; LA artists are particularly well represented.

Around town While Isozaki's museum was under construction, MOCA transformed a spacious warehouse in Little Tokyo into gallery space, now known as the Geffen Contemporary at MOCA. The vast industrial space, with its ramps and girders, is ideal for big installation pieces. Smaller works occupy a maze of galleries overlooked from a mezzanine level. A series of four "context rooms" notes major historical, political and artistic developments since the 1940s. Across town is a third gallery at the Pacific Design Center (8687 Melrose Avenue, West Hollywood).

THE BASICS

MOCA
www.moca.org
🚏 L6
✉ 250 S. Grand Avenue
☎ 213/626-6222
🕐 Mon, Fri 11–5, Thu 11–8, Sat–Sun 11–6. Closed Tue, Wed and national hols
🍽 Patinette at MOCA
🚌 DASH B
♿ Good
💲 Moderate; free on Thu

Geffen Contemporary
🚏 N7
✉ 152 N. Central Avenue
🚌 DASH A

Natural History Museum of LA County

Dinosaur skeletons (middle) and the beautiful stained-glass dome (right)

THE BASICS

www.nhm.org
+ K8
✉ 900 Exposition Boulevard
☎ 213/763-3466
🕐 Mon–Fri 9.30–5, Sat–Sun 10–5. Closed July 4, Thanksgiving, Christmas, New Year's Day
🍴 Cafeteria
🚌 38, DASH F/Expo Park
♿ Very good
💷 Moderate

HIGHLIGHTS

● Insect zoo
● Dueling dinosaurs in Dinosaur Hall
● Megamouth, the rarest shark in the world
● Shreiber Hall of Birds

Enjoy a collection that dates back 400 million years at this imaginatively designed museum, which also houses engaging exhibits from California's and LA's more recent past.

The broad picture The Natural History Museum of LA County is a handsome Spanish Renaissance Revival affair on the north side of Exposition Park. Its wide-ranging collections cover not only natural history but also superb Mesoamerican artifacts including gold jewelry and pottery from the Maya, Inca and Aztec cultures; an excellent Native American Indian section with a re-created pueblo, intricate Plains Indian beadwork and Navajo textiles; and California and American history galleries.

Natural wonders The museum is big on fossils and dinosaurs. This is the place to ogle a *Sauropod*, a pin-headed 72ft-long (22m) giant and one of the largest dinosaurs ever discovered. It probably weighed around 30–40 tons, dwarfing *Tyrannosaurus rex* (a mere 50ft/15m) long and 6–7 tons). *Carnotaurus*, the meat-eating monster first discovered in Patagonia in 1984, also puts in an appearance, as does the rhino-like Brontops, or "Thunderbeast." On the geological front, there is a glittering Hall of Gems and Minerals. In the Discovery Center there are imaginative touchy-feely games and toys, fossil rubbings and other hands-on diversions. On the mezzanine level, the Insect Zoo offers a creepy-crawly collection including huge hissing cockroaches from Madagascar, pink-toed tarantulas and nauseating assassin bugs.

Flowers at a market
stall (left); the band-
stand in the Old Plaza
(right)

El Pueblo de Los Angeles

Angelenos tend to be snooty about the touristy Olvera Street market, but Sunday's mariachi masses in the Old Plaza Church are worthwhile, as are the more conventional historic sights.

LA's historic heart The site of the original 1781 pueblo settlement covers just a handful of city blocks, yet within its confines are 27 historic buildings, including two museums, restaurants, stores and a Mexican street market. The main thoroughfare is pedestrianized Olvera Street, leading off La Placita, the former town plaza shaded by Moreton Bay fig trees. On the south side of the plaza is the original 1884 Firehouse No. 1, which displays antique firefighting equipment. The Old Plaza Church, on the west side, is the city's oldest Catholic church, dedicated in 1822.

Sterling support Olvera Street fell into disrepair around the turn of the 19th century when the downtown area moved south. By 1926, it was a grimy alley until local civic leader Christine Sterling stepped in. Her campaign to rescue the historic buildings and inaugurate the market is illustrated in a display at the restored Avila Adobe.

Mexican marketplace Across the street, the Visitor Center in the 1887 Sepulveda House distributes walking tour maps; free guided walking tours leave from the Visitor Center. The market is still going strong, and the crowded thoroughfare is bursting with stalls selling everything from Mexican pottery and leatherware to sombreros.

THE BASICS

www.olvera-street.com

Visitor Center
➕ L6
✉ W-12 Olvera Street
☎ 213/628-1274
🕐 Daily 9–4. Olvera Street: daily 10–7. Closed major hols
🚇 DASH B, D
♿ Few
💲 Free
❓ Walking tours Wed–Sat 10–12

Museums
🕐 Avila Adobe: summer daily 9–5, winter 10–4. Firehouse: Tue–Sun 10–3
💲 Free

HIGHLIGHTS

● Authentic, first-rate Mexican food
● *Tropical America*, a mural by Mexican artist David Siqueiros
● Dia de los Muertos festivities

More to See

ANGELS FLIGHT RAILWAY

From 1901 to 1969 the world's shortest railway (total length 315ft/96m) ferried passengers up and down Bunker Hill. Today the historic funicular is again shuttling between Hill Street and California Plaza.

➕ L6 ✉ Hill Street at 4th Street
☎ 213/626-1901 ⏰ Re-opening 2007
🚌 DASH A, B, C 💵 Inexpensive

BRADBURY BUILDING

In 1892 elderly mining millionaire Lewis Bradbury commissioned George Wyman to create a monument to his achievements. The resulting building is remarkable mainly for its soaring, light-filled atrium. Intricate, black wrought-iron railings edge the balconies.

➕ L6 ✉ 304 S. Broadway (access to hallway only) ☎ 213/687-0966 ⏰ Mon–Fri 9–6, Sat–Sun 9–5 🚌 DASH D 🚇 Civic Center 💵 Free

BROADWAY HISTORIC THEATER DISTRICT

For movie fans with an interest in the early days, downtown Broadway is the place to find the movie palaces of yesteryear. Several, such as the Los Angeles (No. 615), the Palace (No. 630) and the Orpheum Theater (No. 842), are still open.

➕ L7 ✉ Broadway, between 3rd and 9th streets 🚇 Pershing Square 🚌 DASH E, 2, 3, 4, 30, 31, 40, 45, 46, 48, 68, 302, 304, 345, 340 💵 Moderate ℹ LA Conservancy

CALIFORNIA SCIENCE CENTER

Hands-on science, technology and environmental displays designed to appeal to children, plus an IMAX theater.

➕ K8 ✉ 700 State Drive, Exposition Park ☎ 323/724-3623 ⏰ Daily 10–5 🚌 DASH F/Expo Park 💵 Free (except IMAX theater)

CATHEDRAL OF OUR LADY OF THE ANGELS

Spanish architect José Rafael Moneo designed this cathedral, which was completed in 2002 to the tune of nearly $190 million (it was built to replace another cathedral that had been severely damaged in the 1994 earthquake). The angular, terra-cotta colored building contains a vast

Bradbury Building

Angels Flight funicular

Dobson pipe organ; note the tapestries along the nave and behind the altar.
➕ L6 ✉ 555 W. Temple Street ☎ 213/680-5200 🚌 Dash B

CITY HALL
This monolith, the tallest building in the city from 1928 to 1959 and "destroyed" in *War of the Worlds*, is familiar as the Daily Planet building in the Superman TV series, and has starred in many other TV shows and films.
➕ L6 ✉ 200 N. Spring Street ☎ 213/978-0600 🚇 Civic Center 🚌 DASH A, B, D

EXPOSITION PARK ROSE GARDEN
This fragrant open site boasts around 20,000 rose bushes from some 200 varieties in a sunken garden beside the Natural History Museum.
➕ K8 ✉ 900 Exposition Boulevard 🚌 DASH F/Expo Park

JAPANESE AMERICAN NATIONAL MUSEUM
The story of Japanese migration to the US, and the Japanese-Americans'

struggle for acceptance in their adopted home. Moving exhibits deal with World War II internment camps.
➕ L6 ✉ 369 E. 1st Street ☎ 213/625-0414 🕐 Tue–Sun 11–5 (Thu until 8) 🚌 DASH A 🖐 Moderate

RICHARD J. RIORDAN CENTRAL LIBRARY
This 1926 Beaux Arts treasure is ornamented with carved reliefs of great thinkers, writers, scientists and choice *bons mots*.
➕ L6 ✉ 630 W. 5th Street ☎ 213/228-7000 🕐 Mon–Thu 10–8, Fri–Sat 10–6, Sun 1–5. Tours Mon–Fri 12.30, Sat 11, 2, Sun 2 🚇 Pershing Square 🚌 DASH A, B, C, F 🖐 Free

UNION STATION
With a Spanish Mission-style design by J. and D. Parkinson, the station was built by the railroad companies in 1939. View the lofty, barrel-shaped ceiling and Moorish tile trim of the main hall.
➕ L6 ✉ 800 N. Alameda Street 🚌 DASH B, D 🚇 Metro Red Line

Waiting area in Union Station

City Hall

Grand Avenue to Olvera Street

From a new cathedral to an old Mexican market, this tour includes a dozen Downtown highlights.

DISTANCE: 1.5 miles (2.5km) **ALLOW:** 3 hours

START

CATHEDRAL OF OUR LADY OF THE ANGELS
🕂 L6 🚌 DASH B

END

OLVERA STREET
🕂 N6 🚌 DASH B, D

WALK

DOWNTOWN

❶ Start at the Cathedral of Our Lady of the Angels (▷ 60). Wander around the 2.5-acre (1ha) plaza, and then venture inside to see the tapestries lining the nave and the gigantic organ.

❽ Enjoy the historic buildings, restaurants and pedestrian-only Olvera Street (▷ 59), a Mexican street market.

❷ Walk south on Grand Avenue, passing the Ahmanson Theatre and the Mark Taper Forum en route to the Walt Disney Concert Hall (Music Center, ▷ 64). Visit the Frank Gehry-designed structure.

❼ Continue north on Broadway to 1st Street. Take a right turn to Spring Street to see imposing City Hall (▷ 61). Continue walking north on Spring Street, right on Aliso Street, and left on N. Main Street to reach El Pueblo de Los Angeles (▷ 59).

❸ Continue down Grand. You'll pass the Museum of Contemporary Art (▷ 56–57), and just across 3rd Street is the top of the city's glass-canyoned Financial District.

❻ Walk through the market and cross Broadway to the Bradbury Building (▷ 60), near the corner of 3rd Street. The building appeared in *Blade Runner* and other films.

❹ The Wells Fargo History Museum is on your right, and California Plaza on your left. Stop at the Plaza to watch the dancing fountains before taking the Angels Flight funicular (▷ 60) from Bunker Hill to Grand Central Market (▷ 52–53).

❺ Wander through the market, which is a great spot to get authentic, Mexican food at a take-out stall.

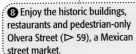

Shopping

505 FLOWER

This square city block between Flower Street and Figueroa Street and 5th Street and 6th Street is anchored by two 52-story towers, with a spectacular fountain in between. There are dozens of retail and specialty shops and restaurants underground between the two towers.
🚇 L6 ✉ 505 S. Flower Street 🚌 10

CASA DE SOUSA

This shop on Olvera Street is known for its Mexican and Central American folk arts, especially the lustrous Oaxacan vases. There's also a gallery exhibiting work by local artists, and great cappuccino.
🚇 L6 ✉ 19 Olvera Street 🚌 DASH B, D

CHUNG KING ROAD

An *L.A. Weekly* art critic called this pedestrian alley LA's East Village. It's loaded with art galleries and also gift shops selling Chinese souvenirs. The galleries coordinate group art openings.
🚇 L6 ✉ Between Yale and Hill streets 🚌 DASH B

CIRRUS GALLERY

Founded in 1971, Cirrus is one of the first art dealers in Downtown, near Little Tokyo and Geffen Contemporary at MOCA. It exhibits works by new and emerging artists, from all over the US and

Europe but especially from southern California. There's also a range of gifts designed by artists and a bookstore.
🚇 L6 ✉ 542 S. Alameda Street 🚌 213/680-3473
🚌 DASH B

FLOWER MART

Two large buildings make up the Flower Mart, in LA's Flower District. Look for basics like roses and tulips, or more unusual plants. Come early for the best selection.
🚇 L7 ✉ 754 Wall Street 🚌 213/627-3696 🚌 DASH E

FREAKS

In Downtown's Arts District, this vintage clothing store sells used Levis, novelty T-shirts, Western shirts, and more.
🚇 L7 ✉ 826 E. 3rd Street 🚌 213/628-1234 🚌 DASH A

THE GARMENT DISTRICT

Downtown's Garment District is a great spot for bargain hunters. Focused around Los Angeles Street (between 8th and 11th streets), it offers dozens of discount retail, jobber and manufacturers' outlet stores with fashion buys at bargain prices. Check out the Cooper Building, one of southern California's largest outlet and discount fashion centers, at 860 Los Angeles Street, with more than 50 labels spread over six floors.

MCMANUS AND MORGAN

Purveyor of an intriguing selection of handmade paper, including marbled paper and papyrus, Mexican paper made from bark, and Nepalese paper made from rice and grass. Also stationery.
🚇 L6 ✉ 2506 W. 7th Street 🚌 213/387-4433 🚌 DASH E

SANTEE ALLEY

In the heart of LA's Garment District, Santee Alley is the place to come for knockoffs of designer shoes and clothing at really low prices. You can pick up fabric and accessories as well as clothing. The first Friday of every month the California Mart (910 S. Los Angeles Street) has sample sales.
🚇 L7 ✉ Between Santee and Maple streets and Olympic Boulevard and 12th Street
🚌 DASH E

SEVENTH & FIG

Relatively modest open-air Downtown mall with a brace of department stores and a food court.
🚇 L6 ✉ 735 S. Figueroa Street 🚌 213/955-7150
🚌 DASH A, E, F

ST. VINCENT JEWELRY CENTER

Hundreds of vendors sell their wares, from platinum and diamonds to inexpensive beads.
🚇 L6 ✉ 650 S. Hill Street 🚌 213/629-2124 🕐 9.30–5.30; closed Sunday 🚇 Metro Red Line 🚌 DASH B, C

Entertainment and Nightlife

BORDELLO
Once a legal bordello and the oldest bar Downtown, this spot harkens back to its mischievous roots with a red interior and burlesque nights. Live music also includes jazz on Sunday.
➕ L6 ✉ 901 E. 1st Street ☎ 213/687-3766 🚌 DASH A, D

BROADWAY BAR
It's dark and noisy throughout this nearly 4,000sq ft (360sq m) spot next to the Orpheum. Enjoy the circular bar, the jukebox, and the patio (for smokers).
➕ L7 ✉ 830 S. Broadway ☎ 213/614-9909 🚌 DASH D

CLUB 740
This recently remodeled club features a state-of-the-art sound system, three levels of music, and several VIP rooms.
➕ L7 ✉ 740 S. Broadway ☎ 213/627-6277 🚌 DASH D, E

GOLDEN GOPHER
The masterminds behind Liquid Kitty in West LA (▷ 81) transformed this dive into a hipster destination. A large patio and classic arcade games.
➕ L7 ✉ 417 W. 8th Street ☎ 213/614-8001 🚌 DASH D

JAPAN AMERICA THEATER
Performances of contemporary and traditional Japanese Noh plays and Kabuki theater.
➕ L6 ✉ 244 S. San Pedro Street, Little Tokyo ☎ 213/680-3700 🚌 DASH A

MAYAN
A fashionably dressy crowd swings to salsa and disco in an exotic former theater downtown.
➕ L7 ✉ 1038 S. Hill Street ☎ 213/746-4287 🚌 DASH D

MUSIC CENTER
LA's chief performing arts complex includes the Dorothy Chandler Pavilion, the Ahmanson Theatre (musicals, drama and comedy), the Mark Taper Forum (drama and occasional music) and the Frank Gehry-designed Walt Disney Concert Hall (home to the LA Philharmonic's winter season). It is also used by the Los Angeles Opera and Los Angeles Chorale.
➕ L6 ✉ 135 N. Grand Avenue ☎ 213/972-7211 🚇 Civic Center 🚌 DASH A, B

REDWOOD BAR & GRILL
Jolly Rogers, rum barrels, rope ladders and other pirate touches dominate here. Regular pub staples like fish-and-chips.
➕ L6 ✉ 316 W. 2nd Street ☎ 213/680-2600 🚇 Metro Red Line 🚌 DASH A, D

ROOF BAR AT THE STANDARD DOWNTOWN
This poolside lounge is still the place to be seen, with its white walls, bright accents and tasty bar menu.
➕ L6 ✉ 550 S. Flower Street ☎ 213/892-8080 🚌 DASH A, B, C, F

STAPLES CENTER
Fabulous sports and entertainment venue, owned by sports and entertainment presenters AEG. This is the home base of the Lakers and Clippers (basketball), Sparks (women's basketball), Kings (ice hockey) and Avengers (football) teams.
➕ K7 ✉ 1111 S. Figueroa Street ☎ 213/742-7340 🚇 Pico/LA Convention Center 🚌 81, 381

HIP HOTEL BARS
The Standard Downtown doesn't have a lock on hotel bars in the area. Consider the upscale Checkers Lounge at Hilton Checkers (535 S. Grand Avenue), cocktails and weekend jazz at the swanky Gallery Bar in the Millennium Biltmore (506 S. Grand Avenue), or the stylish Veranda Bar at Figueroa Hotel (939 S. Figueroa Street). For a more casual drink, visit the Bonaventure Hotel's fourth- floor brewery (404 S. Figueroa Street), which draws an after-work crowd.

Restaurants

PRICES

Prices are approximate, based on a 3-course meal for one person.
$$$$ over $50
$$$ $30–$50
$$ $15–$30
$ under $15

CHECKERS ($$$)
Business-oriented by day, more romantic by night, this top restaurant serves creative pastas, salads and other delights, to be washed down with fine California wines.
➕ L6 ✉ 535 S. Grand Avenue ☎ 213/891-0519 🕐 Breakfast, lunch, dinner daily 🚌 DASH B, E

EMPRESS PAVILION ($$)
Huge, busy and ornate restaurant where throngs gather for myriad morsels of Hong Kong-style dim sum, and house specials.
➕ L6 ✉ 988 N. Hill Street ☎ 213/617-9898 🕐 Breakfast, lunch, dinner daily 🚌 DASH B

LA GOLONDRINA ($$)
Classic Mexican joint in El Pueblo. Mariachi musicians and margaritas.
➕ L6 ✉ W-17 Olvera Street ☎ 213/628-4349 🚇 Union Station 🚌 DASH B

MANDARIN DELI ($)
Chinese dim sum and noodle dishes every which way. No credit cards.
➕ L6 ✉ 727 N. Broadway ☎ 213/623-6054 🚌 DASH B

ORIGINAL PANTRY CAFÉ ($)
Owned by ex-mayor Riordan, this no-nonsense spot serves hearty food on wood tables.
➕ L6 ✉ 877 S. Figueroa Street ☎ 213/972-9279 🚌 81

PACIFIC DINING CAR ($$$)
This railroad-theme restaurant offers superb steaks around the clock. Good selection of fish and shellfish. Also in Santa Monica.
➕ K6 ✉ 1310 W. 6th Street ☎ 213/483-6000 🕐 24 hours daily 🚌 18, 53

PATINA ($$$)
With a move from Melrose to Downtown, Patina now serves its exceptional modern French cuisine in a space adjoining the Walt Disney Concert Hall.
➕ L6 ✉ 141 S. Grand Avenue ☎ 213/972-3331

MALLS AND MARKETS

LA's numerous shopping malls, such as the Beverly Center (▷ 40) and downtown's Seventh Marketplace are a good source of cheap eats, offering a wide choice of fast-food outlets as well as delis and ethnic take-out counters with shared seating. The down-to-earth Grand Central Market (▷ 52–53) is the best place to find budget bites downtown bar none.

🕐 Lunch, dinner daily 🚌 10, 11

PHILIPPE THE ORIGINAL ($)
Crusty fried bread, French dip sandwiches piled high with meats, cheese and extra-hot mustard. Heroic breakfasts and homemade pies.
➕ L6 ✉ 1001 N. Almeda Street ☎ 213/628-3781 🚇 Union Station 🚌 DASH B

SEOUL JUNG ($$$)
Exquisite Korean cuisine, including traditional barbecue prepared at the table. Luxurious surroundings and solicitous service.
➕ L6 ✉ Wilshire Grand Hotel, 930 Wilshire Boulevard ☎ 213/688-7880 🕐 Lunch, dinner daily 🚌 18, 20, 21, 200

THOUSAND CRANES ($$$)
Fine Japanese cuisine, sushi and tempura counters, charming service and views over a Japanese garden.
➕ L6 ✉ New Otani Hotel, 120 S. Los Angeles Street, Little Tokyo ☎ 213/253-9255 🕐 Lunch Sun–Fri, dinner daily 🚌 DASH A

WATER GRILL ($$$)
Renowned seafood restaurant with oyster bar.
➕ L6 ✉ 544 S. Grand Avenue ☎ 213/891-0900 🕐 Lunch, dinner Mon–Fri; dinner Sat, Sun 🚌 DASH B, E

A collection of neighborhoods with distinct personalities, the Westside includes in-vogue Culver City and collegiate Westwood and the beachside communities of Santa Monica and Venice Beach.

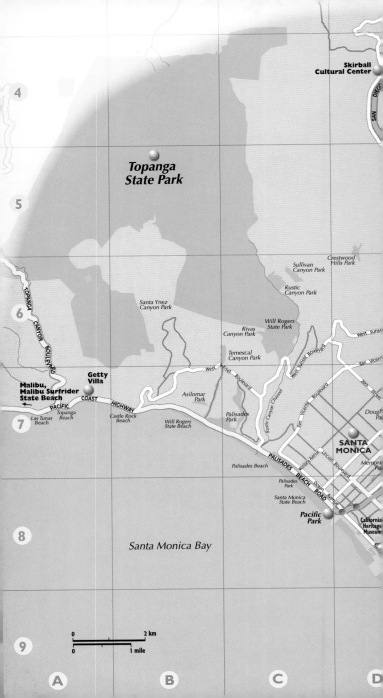

4

Skirball
Cultural Center

5

*Topanga
State Park*

Crestwood
Hills Park

Sullivan
Canyon Park

Rustic
Canyon Park

6

Santa Ynez
Canyon Park

Rivas
Canyon Park

Will Rogers
State Park

West Sunset

West Sunset Boulevard

San Vicente

Temescal
Canyon Park

West Sunset Boulevard

Rustic Canyon Channel

San Vicente Boulevard

26th Street

Getty
Villa

West Sunset Boulevard

Dough
Pa

**Malibu,
Malibu Surfrider
State Beach**

PACIFIC

COAST HIGHWAY

Asilomar
Park

**SANTA
MONICA**

*Las Tunas
Beach*

Topanga
Beach

Castle Rock
Beach

Will Rogers
State Beach

Palisades
Park

Montana Avenue

Lincoln Boulevard

Memor
Pa

7

PALISADES BEACH ROAD

Palisades Beach

Palisades
Park

Santa Monica
State Beach

Ocean Avenue

California
Heritage
Museum

*Pacific
Park*

8

Santa Monica Bay

TOPANGA CANYON BOULEVARD

SAN DIEGO

0   2 km

0   1 mile

9

A   **B**   **C**   **D**

FREEWAY

Mulholland Drive

Stone
Canyon
Reservoir

North Sepulveda Boulevard

North Beverly Glen Boulevard

West Sunset Boulevard

**Getty
Center**

**Franklin D Murphy
Sculpture Garden**

West Sunset Boulevard

South Sepulveda Boulevard

SAN DIEGO FREEWAY

**University
of California-
Los Angeles**

South Beverly Glen Boulevard

Wilshire Boulevard

Boulevard

**UCLA Hammer
Museum**

SANTA MONICA BOULEVARD

Westwood Boulevard

Westwood Boulevard

West Olympic Boulevard

*Westwood
Park*

Boulevard

*Brentwood
Park*

Wilshire Boulevard

SANTA MONICA BOULEVARD

South Sepulveda Boulevard

Olympic Boulevard

Street

SANTA MONICA FREEWAY

Sawtelle Boulevard

**Museum
of Flying**

South Bundy Drive

*Clover
Park*

Park Boulevard

**Santa Monica
Municipal**

Ocean Park Boulevard

LINCOLN BOULEVARD

Venice Boulevard

Boulevard

Washington Boulevard

*Admiralty
Park*

MARINA FREEWAY

Venice Boulevard

Pacific Avenue

Marina del Rey

**Venice
Beach**

Grand Canal

Way

E   **F**   **G**

Getty Center

The five pavilions of the Getty Center house extraordinary works of art

HIGHLIGHTS

- Ludwig Manuscripts
- Old Master Gallery
- French decorative arts
- *Irises*, Van Gogh

TIPS

- Free 1-hour gallery tours take place three times a day.
- Free architecture tours are five times a day.

Carved into the foothills of West LA's Santa Monica Mountains, Richard Meier's magnificent Getty Center impresses visitors with its breathtaking architecture, city views and art.

Background Oil billionaire J. Paul Getty began collecting in the 1930s and a passion for Greek and Roman antiquities inspired the J. Paul Getty Museum in Malibu (▷ 71). After his death in 1976 and his $700 million bequest, the size of its collections swelled. Opened in 1997, the $1 billion Getty Center houses Western art from the Middle Ages to the present as well as the J. Paul Getty Trust's arts, education, research and funding projects.

Treasure Part fortress, part piazza, and focus of the 24-acre (10ha) complex, the inside-out architecture is a triumph. Five honey-colored pavilions flank the central courtyard. The first four display the collections in chronological order; decorative arts and sculpture are on the first floor and paintings from the corresponding period on the upper level; the fifth pavilion houses special exhibitions.

Art First you will see medieval and Renaissance works, from illuminated manuscripts to the works of Fra Angelico. Next, stroll by the Old Masters, including Titian, Brueghel and Rembrandt. There are also splendid English portraits, grand galleries of 18th-century French decorative arts, 19th and 20th century photographs—and Van Gogh's *Irises*. Step outside to the outdoor café or to explore the elegant geometric plantings in the garden.

Getty Villa

The Getty Villa in Malibu reopened in January 2006 after a major overhaul. This cultural landmark vividly evokes the classical world in its landscape and architecture.

Background Constructed in the early 1970s, the Getty Villa underwent a facelift after the opening of the stunning Getty Center (▷ 70). The Malibu site closed for eight years (many years longer than initially expected), but reopened to great fanfare. No expense was spared for the new Villa, which now houses more than 44,000 antiquities of Greek, Roman, and Etruscan origin. The building resembles an ancient Roman villa—appropriately enough, as it is dedicated to Greek, Roman and Etruscan antiquities.

Layout Visitors to the Villa walk through an open-air pavilion and then meander down a pathway to an impressive 450-seat outdoor classical theater. From the theater, visitors can enter the galleries or have lunch or a snack in the new café. Twenty-three galleries display permanent works from the collection, while six galleries showcase changing exhibitions. Antiquity, of course, is always the underlying theme.

Art More than 1,200 objects on display here range from the rare—*Victorious Youth*, aka the Getty Bronze, which is kept in a climate-controlled room—to the ordinary. Or rather, items that would have been ordinary to these ancient peoples, such as coins, vases and necklaces. The works date from 6,500BC to AD400.

THE BASICS

www.getty.edu

➕ A7

✉ 17985 Pacific Coast Highway, Pacific Palisades (access from northbound only)

☎ 310/440-7300

🕐 Thu–Mon 10–5. Closed national hols

🍴 Café; pre-order picnic lunches also available

🚌 534. You must have your advance admission ticket punched by the driver to enter the Villa

♿ Excellent

👤 Museum free, but you need an advance, timed ticket. Parking moderate (reservations essential)

❓ Audio guides, talks, concerts

HIGHLIGHTS

● Bronze *Victorious Youth* statue, *c*300–100BC
● Herb garden and Outer Peristyle
● Performances in the outdoor classical theater

Rent a bicycle (opposite), ride the waves (left) or relax in the shade of palm trees (right)

Santa Monica and Malibu

Tanned bodies playing volleyball, the crowded bicycle path, plus great shopping and drinking on the bustling promenade draw crowds to this enduringly popular stretch of coast.

Pier pressure Santa Monica's landmark 1909 pier still exudes an old-fashioned amusement-park aura that evokes a fuzzy nostalgia in adults and requests for money from attendant offspring. Along the weathered wooden boardwalk, Pacific Park's (▷ 77) giant Ferris wheel and roller coaster loom above the restored 1922 carousel operated by Paul Newman in *The Sting*. Down at beach level, the UCLA Ocean Discovery Center presents marine exhibits, aquariums and touch tanks. You can also rent a bicycle or in-line skates to swoop along the 26-mile (42km) concrete beach path.

Beyond the beach Santa Monica's inland entertainment hub is Third Street Promenade, four pedestrian-only blocks of stores, cafés and movie theaters. For a more esoteric experience, check out Main Street (between Hollister and Rose avenues), with its restaurants and galleries, and the California Heritage Museum at Ocean Park.

Along the coast Quieter and more remote than Santa Monica, its southern neighbor, the lovely enclave of Malibu, lures visitors with its 27 miles (43km) of sprawling beaches and canyons. Despite its drawbacks—traffic, brush fires and mud slides—plenty of Hollywood luminaries hang their hats here. The real draw, though, is the surfing.

THE BASICS

www.santamonica.com
Santa Monica ✚ D7
Malibu ✚ Off map, west of A7

✉ Santa Monica Visitor Center: 1920 Main Street, Suite B (☎ 310/393-7593, ⏰ Daily 9–6). Also kiosk at 1400 Ocean Avenue (between Santa Monica Boulevard and Colorado Avenue ⏰ Daily 10–4, 9–5 in summer)

🍴 Restaurants, bars and cafés

🚌 SM1, 2, 4, 7, 8, 9, 10

♿ Good to nonexistent depending on location

❓ Malibu surfing reports:
☎ 310/457-9701

HIGHLIGHTS

- Natural Elements Sculpture Park
- Pacific Coast Bicycle Path
- Santa Monica Pier
- Sunset from Palisades Park, on Ocean Avenue, by Santa Monica and Wilshire boulevards
- Third Street Promenade

HIGHLIGHTS

- Muscle Beach
- Ocean Front Walk
- Venice Canal Walkway (access from S. Venice Boulevard)
- Venice Boardwalk
- Venice Pier

TIP

- The sky is often overcast in the mornings, especially in spring and early summer, so save your trip to the beach until the afternoon.

Best known for its beachfront boardwalk, bohemian Venice Beach also has a flourishing artists' community, lovely outdoor dining and recreational facilities. People-watching is the number one pastime.

The action Where Main crosses Rose Street, Joseph Borofsky's *Ballerina Clown* figure greets visitors to Venice. It is an appropriate icon for this entertaining beach community, a throwback to the psychedelic '60s combined with the narcissism of Muscle Beach. Ocean Front Walk is where it all hangs out, a nonstop parade of scantily clad humanity, shiny bodybuilders, funky street performers, tourists and bustling market stalls.

Italian dream Developer Abbot Kinney created this American snapshot of Venice, Italy, in the early

There's more to Venice Beach than sand and sea: street performers, market stalls, artists, rollerbladers, dog walkers and tourists

1900s as a tribute to its European counterpart, and the Venice Canal Walkway, just inland from Ocean Front Walk, explores the quiet, canal-lined residential neighborhood that gave the area its name. Venice, California, has earned itself both starring roles and bit parts in various films—as the seedy backdrop in Orson Welles' *Touch of Evil*, for example, and as the home of the fictitious Rydell High in the 1970s musical film *Grease*, starring John Travolta and Olivia Newton-John.

Join the buzz Energetic visitors should consider renting a bicycle or a pair of Rollerblades to join the masses on Ocean Front Walk. Afterward, take a stroll down Main Street, the artery that connects Santa Monica and Venice, and check out the shops, buildings and art galleries. Crowds flock to the area, but do exercise caution at night.

THE BASICS

✚ D9
☎ Venice Chamber of Commerce: 310/822-5425; info@venicechamber.net
🚌 SM1, SM2, SM3
♿ Good to nonexistent depending on location

UCLA Hammer Museum

The Hammer Museum has been criticized for its architecture, among other things

THE BASICS

www.hammer.ucla.edu
🔁 E6
✉ 10899 Wilshire Boulevard, Westwood
☎ 310/443-7000
🕐 Tue–Sat 11–7 (Thu until 9), Sun 11–5. Closed national hols
🍴 Courtyard café
🚌 20, 21, 22, 302, 305
♿ Very good
💵 Inexpensive (free Thu)

HIGHLIGHTS

● *Beach at Trouville*, Boudin
● *Dans l'Omnibus*, Vuillard
● Grunwald Center exhibitions
● *Hospital at Saint-Rémy*, Van Gogh
● *Mme Hessel at the Seashore*, Vuillard
● *The Sower*, Van Gogh
● *Boy Resting*, Cézanne

Criticized for its architecture, the lack of "importance" of its collections, even for its existence, the Hammer does have several small-scale treasures, plus the new, state-of-the-art Billy Wilder Theater.

Hammer and tongs Much of the highbrow carping about the Hammer is probably based on the general dislike of Armand Hammer himself. The immensely rich and acquisitive oil millionaire originally promised his art collections to a number of local institutions. To their chagrin, he then decided to build his own museum instead.

Minor miracles Modest in size, the Hammer is a respite from more overwhelming local museums. Its collection is composed mainly of Impressionist and Postimpressionist works by painters such as Monet, Pissarro and Mary Cassatt; complementary works from UCLA's own collections are also shown here.

Changing exhibitions Selections from the 19th-century "Daumier and His Contemporaries Collection," with paintings, sculpture and lithographs by the leading French satirist of the age, are shown in rotation. The museum is also a showcase for the UCLA Grunwald Center for the Graphic Arts. This collection of more than 35,000 prints, drawings, photographs and book illustrations, including works by Dürer, Cézanne, Matisse and Jasper Johns, is displayed in other themed exhibitions.

FRANKLIN D. MURPHY SCULPTURE GARDEN

Sculptures by such artists as Arp, Hepworth and Calder are sprinkled liberally over sunny lawns shaded by jacaranda trees. Works by Jacques Lipchitz, Henry Moore, Alexander Calder, Maillol and Rodin can be found on the tree-lined promenade.

➕ E6 ✉ UCLA Campus off Circle Drive East, Westwood 🕐 Open site 🚌 2, 302, SM1, 2, 3, 8, 12 (off Sunset Boulevard)

MALIBU SURFRIDER STATE BEACH

One of California's original surfing beaches offers year-round waves but the best are during the late summer.

➕ Off map, west of A7 ✉ Off Pacific Coast Highway, Malibu 🚌 434

PACIFIC PARK

Seaside fairground with traditional rides, sideshows and virtual reality simulator adventures.

➕ C8 ✉ Santa Monica Pier ☎ 310/260-8744 🕐 Seasonal schedule 🚌 20, 22, 33, SM1, 7, 8, 10 ✋ Charge per ride

SKIRBALL CULTURAL CENTER

This spacious museum near the Getty Center explores the relationship between 4,000 years of Jewish culture and modern life in America. There is also a Discovery Center with hands-on activities.

➕ D4 ✉ 2701 N. Sepulveda Boulevard ☎ 310/440-4500 🕐 Tue, Wed, Fri, Sat 12–5, Thu 12–9, Sun 11–5 🚌 561, SM14 ✋ Moderate; free Thu

TOPANGA CANYON

Topanga State Park covers more than 12,000 acres (52sq km) and is a great place to go hiking within reach of the city. Topanga Creek runs through Topanga Canyon, a scenic part of the state park that became popular with artists and hippies since blacklisted *Waltons* actor Will Geer set up home here in the 1950s. Topanga Community House was once used for concerts by residents like The Byrds and Neil Young but is now used mainly for children's entertainment.

➕ A5, B5 ✉ Topanga Canyon Boulevard west of Pacific Palisades, east of Malibu

WEST LA ★ **MORE TO SEE**

Franklin D. Murphy Sculpture Garden

Topanga Canyon

Santa Monica

Great ocean views, pedestrian-only shopping and beachfront people-watching.

DISTANCE: 2 miles (3.2km)   **ALLOW:** 2–3 hours

START

PALISADES PARK
✚ D8 🚌 SM1, SM7, SM8, SM10

END

CASA DEL MAR
✚ D8 🚌 SM7, SM10

1 Start at the south end of Palisades Park, where Colorado Boulevard meets Santa Monica Pier. Head north through the park along the top of the cliffs. On a clear day you can see Catalina Island in the distance.

8 Continue south along the bicycle path until you reach Casa del Mar. The Veranda Bar (▷ 82) there has great views of the ocean.

2 Your route takes you parallel to Ocean Avenue, and on your right you'll pass boulevards that run all the way to downtown LA. When you reach Wilshire Boulevard, turn right.

7 Just south of the volleyball courts on the path is the original Muscle Beach (note the sign) on your right. To your left is a life-size chessboard along with five dozen chessboards (chess pieces available).

3 At Wilshire and 2nd is the historic Miramar Hotel. Continue east and turn right again on 3rd Street to reach Third Street Promenade (▷ 80). Take in the shops, people-watch and grab a bite to eat at one of many cafés.

6 From the Pier take the steps down to the bicycle path. Stop and watch a game of pickup beach volleyball south of the Pier, or rent a bike or Rollerblades.

4 The Promenade dead-ends at Broadway, where you will turn right. Walk back to Ocean Avenue and turn left to reach the Pier.

5 At the Pier, ride the solar-powered Ferris (the only one in the world) or pay 25¢ for binoculars to look at the sea lions and dolphins.

WALK

WEST LA

Shopping

ABBOT KINNEY BOULEVARD

The street, named for the founder of Venice, has a variety of shops, from antique furniture to contemporary galleries to clothing boutiques. The place to visit for home furnishings.

D9 ✉ Abbot Kinney between Westminster and Milwood avenues 🚌 SM1, SM2, 333

BERGAMOT STATION

This old trolley station now houses some 21 contemporary galleries dealing in an exciting range of art, sculpture, furniture and glass, as well as photography.

D7 ✉ 2525 Michigan Avenue, Santa Monica 🚌 SM9

THE BLUE JEANS BAR

An array of the latest hot denim labels, and helpful clerks to help you find the right jeans for your figure.

D7 ✉ 1409 Montana Avenue, Santa Monica ☎ 310/656-7898 🚌 SM3

BORDERS BOOKS AND MUSIC

An impressive selection of classic and contemporary literature and music, plus a handy in-store café.

D8 ✉ 1415 3rd Street Promenade, Santa Monica ☎ 310/393-9290 🚌 4, 20, 21, 22, SM1, 2, 3, 7, 8, 9, 10

BROADWAY GALLERY COMPLEX

Another Santa Monica arts enclave specializing in contemporary paintings, prints and functional art such as furnishings with a distinctive California style.

D7 ✉ 2018–2114 Broadway (between 20th and Cloverfield), Santa Monica 🚌 4, SM1, 10

DEL MANO GALLERY

A terrific array of innovative and affordable contemporary crafts ranging from jewelry to art glass, ceramics and furnishings.

D6 ✉ 11981 San Vicente Boulevard, Brentwood ☎ 310/476-8508 🚌 22, SM3

EVERY PICTURE TELLS A STORY

Captivating bookstore-gallery displaying original art and lithographs from children's books: Eric Carle, Tim Burton, Maurice Sendak.

D7 ✉ 1311C Montana Avenue, Santa Monica ☎ 310/451-2700 🚌 SM3

OCEANFRONT WALK

Looking for LA T-shirts, Dodgers baseball caps, postcards and other souvenirs? Then make a beeline for Venice Beach's open-air bazaar where the stalls are piled high with cheap LA-themed goods, $5 sunglasses, microscopic bikinis, West Coast thrash CDs and New Age tie-dye creations.

FRED SEGAL

This outpost of Fred Segal is a must-visit shopping destination, both for browsing and star sightings.

D8 ✉ 420 Broadway ☎ 310/576-6062 🚌 SM7, SM9

GOTTA HAVE IT

Behind an eye-catching facade with a playing card design, serried ranks of wildly assorted retro wear for guys and gals.

D9 ✉ 1516 Pacific Avenue, Venice Beach ☎ 310/392-5949 🚌 SM7

HEAR MUSIC

Part of Starbucks, this is a small but inviting and user-friendly music store with well-chosen rock, jazz, classical, folk and world music.

D8 ✉ 1429 3rd Street Promenade, Santa Monica ☎ 310/319-9527 🚌 4, 20, 22, SM1, 2, 3, 7, 8, 9, 10

MAIN STREET

Hip boutiques, arty design and novelty shops helpfully interspersed with good restaurants.

D8–D9 ✉ Main Street (between Hollister and Rose avenues), Santa Monica 🚌 SM1, 8, 10

MONTANA AVENUE

Ten blocks of super upscale shopping, designer boutiques, elegant home-decorating emporiums, antique stores and luxurious beauty salons for the

WEST LA

SHOPPING

woman with almost everything.

D7/C7 ✉ Montana Avenue (between 7th and 17th streets), Santa Monica 🚇 SM3

PARIS 1900
Antique garments and linens. Original Victorian and Edwardian collector's pieces for very special occasions. Open by appointment or chance.
D8 ✉ 2703 Main Street, Santa Monica ☎ 310/396-0405 🚇 33, SM1

THE PUZZLE ZOO
Discover an astounding array of puzzles for beginners to pros, as well as action figures and other toys.
D8 ✉ 1413 3rd Street Promenade, Santa Monica ☎ 310/393-9201 🚇 4, 20, 22, SM1, 2, 3, 7, 8, 9, 10

SANTA MONICA OUTDOOR ANTIQUES AND COLLECTABLE MARKET
A bimonthly market where hundreds of vendors sell furniture, jewelry, housewares and other vintage delights.
E8 ✉ Santa Monica Airport ☎ 323/933-2511 🕐 1st and 4th Sun of each month 🚇 SM8

SANTA MONICA PLACE
Three floors of boutiques, accessories, kids' clothes and lingerie, from Macy's to Victoria's Secret, plus a food court.
D8 ✉ Broadway at 3rd

Street, Santa Monica ☎ 310/394-5451 🚇 4, 20, 22, 33, SM1, 2, 3, 7, 8, 9, 10

SMALL WORLD BOOKS & THE MYSTERY ANNEXE
Convenient beachfront emporium: everything from classics and a few foreign-language books to beach-holiday mysteries and sex "n" sun sagas.
D9 ✉ 1407 Ocean Front Walk, Venice Beach ☎ 310/399-2360 🚇 33

THIRD STREET PROMENADE
Shoppers, street musicians and street vendors jostle along the pedestrian-only Promenade with many shopping, dining and entertainment options.
C8, D8 ✉ 3rd Street (between Wilshire Boulevard and Broadway), Santa Monica 🚇 4, 20, 22, SM1, 2, 3, 7, 8, 9, 10

BEACHWEAR
Having the right bathing suit for the beach is key. Wise shoppers in need follow Angelenos to these destinations: Canyon Beachwear (✉ 106 Entrada Drive, Santa Monica ☎ 310/459-5070); Diane's Swimwear (✉ 620 Wilshire Boulevard, Santa Monica ☎ 310/395-3545); and Bikini Islands (✉ 38 Washington Boulevard, Marina Del Rey ☎ 310/306-6901).

VIDIOTS
A fabulous collection of foreign and rare movies, cinema-related books and scripts.
D8 ✉ 302 Pico Boulevard, Santa Monica ☎ 310/392-8508 🚇 SM2, 7

WESTFIELD CENTURY CITY
LA's premier outdoor shopping, dining and entertainment complex, with some 140 stores.
F6 ✉ 10250 Santa Monica Boulevard, West LA ☎ 310/277-3898 🚇 27, 28, 316, 328

WESTSIDE PAVILION
Chic selection of men's and women's fashions, gifts, dining places and movie theaters.
F7 ✉ 10800 W. Pico Boulevard, West LA ☎ 310/474-6255 🚇 SM7, 8, 12, 13

WESTWOOD VILLAGE
Mediterranean-style village of intersecting streets whose fashion, movie theaters and music shops appeal to students from the neighboring UCLA campus. Many cafés.
E6 ✉ Westwood Boulevard (off Wilshire Boulevard), Westwood 🚇 20, 21, 22, 302, 305, SM1, 2, 3, 8, 12

Entertainment and Nightlife

14 BELOW

A Westside club, this unassuming nightspot isn't sleek, but it offers bands playing all types of music, from R&B to rock and alternative. The back room has a pool table.
➕ D7 ✉ 1348 14th Street, Santa Monica ☎ 310/451-5040 🚌 4, SM1

AMF MAR VISTA BOWL

Futuristic, space-age decor and various discounts add to the wholesome fun at this bowling alley.
➕ E9 ✉ 12125 Venice Boulevard, Venice ☎ 310/391-5288 🚌 33

BURKE WILLIAMS DAY SPA & MASSAGE CENTER

Celebrity favorite for hedonistic beauty treatments from facials and pedicures to thermal seaweed wraps.
➕ D8 ✉ 1358 4th Street, Santa Monica ☎ 310/587-3366 🚌 4, 20, 22, SM2

CAMEO BAR AT THE VICEROY

This hotel bar is sleek but not pretentious, with a gray, green, and white color palette, outdoor cabanas for poolside lounging, and $15 valet parking.
➕ D8 ✉ 1819 Ocean Avenue, Santa Monica ☎ 310/260-7500 🚌 SM7, SM10

CARBON

A young crowd comes for nightly DJs spinning an eclectic mix of music; a video streams silent movies. Easy parking.
➕ G7 ✉ 9300 Venice Boulevard, Culver City ☎ 310/558-9302 🚌 33, SM12

CHEZ JAY

Laid-back neighborhood beach bar with a broad clientele. Great jukebox.
➕ D8 ✉ 1657 Ocean Avenue, Santa Monica ☎ 310/395-1741 🚌 20, 22, 33, SM1, 10

CIRCLE BAR

A circular bar and a 20-something crowd, plenty of them on the prowl.
➕ D8 ✉ 2926 Main Street, Santa Monica ☎ 310/450-0508 🚌 SM8, 33, 333

FATHER'S OFFICE

Small, comfortable and noisy spot with 30 beers on draft. More than 50 years in business.

FILM PREMIERES

Celebrities frequently gather for film premieres in Westwood, a hub for single-screen movie theaters like the Mann Bruin (948 Broxton Ave.), the Mann Village (961 Broxton Ave., formerly the Fox Theatre) and the Crest (1262 Westwood Blvd.), built by Frances Fonda, the mother of actors Jane and Peter Fonda.

➕ C7 ✉ 1028 Montana Avenue ☎ 310/393-2337 🚌 SM3

GAS LITE

Dive bar that's open 20 hours a day every day of the year. The small dance floor and karaoke nights draw a young crowd.
➕ D7 ✉ 2030 Wilshire Boulevard ☎ 310/829-2382 🚌 SM2, SM3

GEFFEN PLAYHOUSE

Neighborhood theater with a fine reputation, intimate enough to host one-man shows.
➕ E6 ✉ 10886 Le Conte Avenue ☎ 310/208-5454 🚌 20, 21, 22, SM1, 2, 3, 8, 12

HARVELLE'S

Westside neighborhood bar-cum-terrific blues club.
➕ D8 ✉ 1432 4th Street, Santa Monica ☎ 310/395-1676 🚌 4, SM1, 9, 10

JAZZ BAKERY

Housed in the beloved Helms Bakery building, Culver City's liquor-free jazz spot welcomes patrons of all ages. Pastries and hot beverages are served.
➕ G7 ✉ 3233 Helms Avenue, Culver City ☎ 310/271-9039 🚌 33, 333

LIQUID KITTY

The neighborhood is non-descript, but the martinis and DJs in this dark bar are anything but.
➕ E7 ✉ 11780 W. Pico Boulevard ☎ 310/473-3707 🚌 SM7

MCCABE'S GUITAR SHOP

Guitar shop by day, R&B-rock-jazz-folk showcase on Friday and Saturday nights with some pretty impressive names. Intimate, informal, alcohol-free but tea and cookies available during musical acts.

✚ E7 ✉ 3101 W. Pico Boulevard, Santa Monica ☎ 310/828-4497 🚌 SM7

NUART THEATRE

Top-notch art house theater showing foreign films, indies, documentaries and more. Second branch called the NuWilshire Theatre (1314 Wilshire Boulevard, Santa Monica; tel 310/281-8223).

✚ E7 ✉ 11272 Santa Monica Boulevard, Los Angeles ☎ 310/281-8223 🚌 SM4, 304

ODYSSEY THEATRE

One of the city's most highly regarded avant-garde theater companies offers ensembles and visiting productions.

✚ E7 ✉ 2055 S. Sepulveda Boulevard, West LA ☎ 310/477-2055 🚌 SM9

THE OTHER ROOM

A combination wine bar and brewery, with a great selection of wines by the glass, bottled beer and brews on tap. No food is served, but you can bring in food from local restaurants.

✚ D9 ✉ 1201 Abbot Kinney Boulevard, Venice ☎ 310/396-6230 🚌 SM1, SM2, 333

ROOSTERFISH

A gay bar that's not in West Hollywood, this laid-back Westside hangout offers a jukebox, pool table and video games.

✚ D9 ✉ 1302 Abbot Kinney Boulevard, Venice ☎ 310/392-2123 🚌 SM1, SM2, 333

SAINTS & SINNERS

Cupid makes an appearance at this Culver City lounge, which serves cocktails such as Evil Dewars (Scotch) and Hell Fire (with cinnamon Schnapps).

✚ F8 ✉ 10899 Venice Boulevard, Culver City ☎ 310/842-8066 🚌 33, 333

UCLA CENTER FOR THE PERFORMING ARTS

Also known as Wadsworth Theater, this off-campus facility offers more than 200 music and dance events a year from homegrown and visiting performers.

✚ E6 ✉ 10920 Wilshire Boulevard, Westwood ☎ 310/825-2101 🚌 20, 21, 22, SM2

VERANDA BAR AT CASA DEL MAR

Views of the ocean and the Santa Monica pier don't come cheap, but the comfortable wicker chairs, tons of space, and a soothing pianist help ease the sticker shock.

✚ D8 ✉ 1910 Ocean Way, Santa Monica ☎ 310/581-5533 🚌 SM7, SM10

VODA

A post-work Manhattan-type crowd frequents this vodka bar in Santa Monica.

✚ D8 ✉ 1449 2nd Street, Santa Monica ☎ 310/394-9774 🚌 SM2, 4, 20, 22

WHISKEY BLUE AT THE W

This bar (from Cindy Crawford's husband) exudes an air of pure sophistication with the heat cranked up.

✚ E6 ✉ 930 Hilgard Avenue, Westwood ☎ 310/208-8765 🚌 SM8, SM12

YE OLDE KING'S HEAD

Popular with local Brits. Draft beer, darts, pub grub and heroic English breakfasts.

✚ D8 ✉ 116 Santa Monica Boulevard, Santa Monica ☎ 310/451-1402 🚌 4, 20, 22, 33, SM17, 10

KARAOKE

Practice your vocals in public, or listen to others doing the same, at a bar offering karaoke night. Try Backstage (✉ 10400 Culver Boulevard ☎ 310/839-3892, Thu–Sat) in Culver City or Britannia Pub (✉ 318 Santa Monica Boulevard ☎ 310/458-5350, Tue, Thu, Sat, Sun) in Santa Monica.

Sports and Leisure

AQUA SURF SCHOOL
www.aquasurfschool.com
Choose from private lessons, group lessons (Sunday mornings), and package deals. Available year-round, lessons include surfboard, wetsuit and two hours with an instructor.
ℹ️ Coastal communities
☎ 310/452-SURF

BLUEWATER SAILING
There are many options for you and the Pacific Ocean, including chartering your own boat, taking an island cruise, or taking a private or group sailing lesson.
➕ E9 ✉️ 13505 Bali Way, Marina Del Rey ☎ 310/823-5545 or 866/944-7245
🚌 SM3

CULVER ICE ARENA
You can take a spin on the ice year-round at this indoor rink. Call for public skating hours.
➕ F8 ✉️ 4545 Sepulveda Boulevard, Culver City
☎ 310/398-5719 or 310/398-5718 🚌 734

GOLD'S GYM
Home of the Gold's Gym worldwide body-building empire.
➕ D8 ✉️ 360 Hampton Drive, Venice Beach
☎ 310/392-6004 🚌 33, SM1

LEARN TO SURF LA
www.learntosurfla.com
Year-round surfing lessons for individuals and groups, including adult group lessons on Saturday mornings. Lessons include all equipment.
ℹ️ Coastal communities
☎ 310/663-2479

MALIBU COUNTRY CLUB
Public 18-hole golf course in scenic Malibu. Lessons available. Shirts with a collar required; no denim.
➕ Off map, west ✉️ 901 Encinal Canyon Road, Malibu
☎ 818/889-6680

MALIBU CREEK STATE PARK
Once used as a set for *M*A*S*H* and *Planet of the Apes*, this park has 15 miles (24km) of trails shared by bikers, hikers and horseback riders; swimmers and bird-watchers also welcome.
➕ Off map, west ✉️ 925 Las Virgenes Road
☎ 818/880-0367

MALIBU SURF SHACK
Find surfboards, kayaks, beach chairs and other gear for rent at this shop on PCH.

JOGGING
LA's most attractive option is probably the 22-mile (35km) beach path running south from Santa Monica. Or try Exposition Park downtown; Griffith Park in the Hollywood Hills; and, just to the west, the great trail around quiet Lake Hollywood, reached by car off Cahuenga Boulevard (via Dix Street).

➕ Off map, west ✉️ 22935 Pacific Coast Highway
☎ 310/456-8508

MARINA DEL REY SPORTFISHING
Twilight fishing (May to September), private fishing charters and whale-watching are among the offerings for experienced anglers and newcomers alike. Boats include rod rentals and tackle, bait, fish cleaning and fishing licenses.
➕ E9 ✉️ Dock 52, Fiji Way, Marina del Rey ☎ 310/822-3625 🚌 SM3

PERRY'S CAFÉ & RENTALS
Four branches on Ocean Front Walk rent bikes, Rollerblades, scooters, volleyballs, boogie boards and more. They also lead three-hour bicycle tours.
➕ C8, D8 ✉️ Ocean Front Walk; two north of Pier, two south of Pier, Santa Monica
☎ 310/372-3138

RANCHO PARK GOLF
An 18-hole course in Cheviot Hills that's open to the public.
➕ F6–F7 ✉️ 10460 W. Pico Boulevard, Los Angeles
☎ 310/838-7373 🚌 7

SANTA MONICA MOUNTAINS RECREATION
www.nps.gov/samo
The world's largest urban national park, the recreation area encompasses Topanga and Will Rogers state parks (▷ 77,

84) and 26 ZIP codes in its 153,075 acres (61,974ha). Activities include mountain biking, bird-watching, horseback riding, and whale-watching. Visit the website for directions and more information.

➕ Off map ✉ 401 W. Hillcrest Drive (National Park Visitor Center in Thousand Oaks, north of LA) ☎ 805/370-2301

SANTA MONICA SWIM CENTER

Two heated outdoor pools at Santa Monica College are available for public use. Visit www.smgov.net/aquatics/rec_swim.htm for listings of other public pools on the Westside.

➕ D8 ✉ 2225 16th Street ☎ 310/458-8700 🚌 7

SOLSTICE CANYON PARK

Solstice has one of the finest walking trails in the mountains. Two routes form a convenient loop from the parking area: the gentle 1.5-mile (2.5km) Solstice International Trail, and the connecting Rising Sun Trail, a 3-mile (5km) high chaparral hike.

➕ Off map, west ✉ 3000 Solstice Canyon Road ☎ 805/370-2301 🚌 534

SOUTH BAY BICYCLE TRAIL

This paved bicycle path starts at Will Rogers State Beach and continues for 22 miles (35km), mean-

dering through Santa Monica and Venice en route to Torrance County Beach, where it ends. Most of the trail is on the beach, though a few short stretches are on city streets. There are a number of spots to rent bikes, Rollerblades, and other modes of transportation.

➕ Starts at B7

TENNIS

www.laparks.org
LA Parks operates public tennis courts throughout LA, including 14 courts in Cheviot Hills (2551 Motor Avenue, tel 310/836-8879) and 8 courts in Westwood (1350 Sepulveda Boulevard, tel 310/

SPECTATOR SPORTS

Catch the LA Dodgers (☎ 866/DODGERS) at home at Dodger Stadium, north of Downtown. The LA Lakers (☎ 213/742-7400), the LA Clippers (☎ 213/742-7500) and the LA Kings (☎ 888/546-4752) all play at the Downtown Staples Center (▷ 64). The Los Angeles Angels of Anaheim (☎ 714/634-2000) play at Angel Stadium in Orange Country. College basketball and football are also very popular, particularly the UCLA Bruins (☎ 310/825-2101) and their crosstown rivals, the USC Trojans (☎ 213/740-4687).

575-8299). Hourly rates between $5 and $8, depending on day and time. To reserve in advance, register for a Tennis Reservation Card ($30). See website for more details.

WESTSIDE WORKOUT PILATES

This Pilates studio in Brentwood offers private sessions and sessions for pairs. Beginners must start with a private session to learn the ropes.

➕ E6 ✉ 12012 Wilshire Boulevard, Suite 201, Los Angeles ☎ 310/207-6334 🚌 SM2, SM3, 20

WILL ROGERS STATE HISTORIC PARK

There is plenty of space for kids to run wild and picnic on this 186-acre (75ha) hillside ranch, the Western-style home of the "Cowboy Philosopher." There are house tours, a nature trail and horses, stables and occasional polo games to watch.

➕ C6 ✉ 1501 Will Rogers State Park Road, off Sunset Boulevard ☎ 310/454-8212 🕐 Park: daily 8–sunset. House: daily 10.30–4.30 🚌 2, 302

YOGA WORKS

Run into your favorite celeb as you assume the cobra pose at this Santa Monica studio.

➕ D7 ✉ 2nd floor 1426 Montana Avenue, Santa Monica ☎ 310/393-5150 🚌 SM3

Restaurants

PRICES

Prices are approximate, based on a 3-course meal for one person.
$$$$ over $50
$$$ $30–$50
$$ $15–$30
$ under $15

APPLE PAN ($)

An LA institution with 1950s counter seating, messy hickory burgers and scrumptious apple and berry pies. Always popular at lunchtime.
🕀 F7 ✉ 10801 W. Pico Boulevard, West LA ☎ 310/475-3585 ⏰ Closed Mon 🚌 212

BORDER GRILL ($$)

Great Mexican food with an inventive twist and a loud, eclectic crowd. Always packed.
🕀 D8 ✉ 1445 4th Street, Santa Monica ☎ 310/451-1655 ⏰ Lunch, dinner daily 🚌 4, SM1, 7, 10

LA CACHETTE ($$$)

Nouvelle French preparations lure diners to owner-chef Jean-Francois Meteigner's oasis of calm.
🕀 F6 ✉ 10506 Santa Monica Boulevard, Century City ☎ 310/470-4992 ⏰ Lunch Mon–Fri, dinner daily 🚌 27, 28, 316, 328

CHINOIS ON MAIN ($$$$)

Another bustling and stylish showcase for chef Wolfgang Puck's sensational California-Chinese culinary creations.
🕀 D8 ✉ 2709 Main Street, Santa Monica ☎ 310/392-9025 ⏰ Lunch Wed–Fri, dinner daily 🚌 33, SM1

DRAGO ($$$)

Celestino Drago delivers mouthwatering Italian fare to an affluent crowd at his casual flagship restaurant. Regulars favor the Sicilian dishes.
🕀 D7 ✉ 2628 Wilshire Boulevard, Santa Monica ☎ 310/828-1585 ⏰ Lunch Mon–Fri, dinner daily 🚌 20, 720, SM2

FIGTREE ($$)

Fresh grilled fish and vegetarian dishes served up on a quiet, sunny patio close to the beach.
🕀 D9 ✉ 429 Ocean Front Walk, Venice Beach ☎ 310/392-4937 ⏰ Daily 8–6 🚌 33

FORD'S FILLING STATION ($$$)

Chef-owner Benjamin

SUNDAY BRUNCH

When Sunday rolls around, Angelenos gear up to "do" brunch, which is generally served from around 10 or 11 until 2. Numerous restaurants throughout the city lay on a variation of the combination breakfast and lunch theme with a set-price menu. However, the most popular brunch spots tend to be found on the coast, and patio dining is at a premium.

Ford (son of Harrison) focuses on seasonal ingredients for his New American fare in this loud, industrial space.
🕀 G7 ✉ 9531 Culver Boulevard ☎ 310/202-1470 ⏰ Lunch Mon–Fri, dinner Mon–Sat 🚌 33, SM 12

FRITTO MISTO ($$)

Excellent Italian fare served in a nondescript section of Santa Monica. Prices are affordable, portions are generous and the crowd is lively.
🕀 D8 ✉ 601 Colorado Boulevard, Santa Monica ☎ 310/458-2829 ⏰ Lunch, dinner daily 🚌 SM5, SM9

THE HUMP ($$$)

Dine on unbelievably fresh sashimi, sushi, hot (cooked) specials and sake, while observing the comings and goings at a Santa Monica Airport.
🕀 E8 ✉ 3221 Donald Douglas South Loop ☎ 310/313-0977 ⏰ Tue–Fri lunch, dinner daily 🚌 SM14

INN OF THE 7TH RAY ($$)

Laid-back New Age hangout in lovely setting. Vegetarian and organic menu plus special barbecued chicken.
🕀 A6 ✉ 128 Old Topanga Road, Malibu ☎ 310/455-1311 ⏰ Sat–Sun brunch; Mon–Fri lunch; dinner daily

KATSUYA ($$$)

Philippe Starck designed the ultrastylish Brentwood outpost of this Japanese

hotspot that serves creative sushi in a sleek setting. There's a sushi bar, of course, and an outdoor terrace.
✚ D6 ✉ 11777 San Vicente Boulevard, Brentwood ☎ 310/207-8744 🕐 Lunch, dinner daily 🚌 SM3, SM4

MARIA TEX MEX PLAYA ($$)
Cheery margarita-fueled Tex-Mex cantina on the beach at Pacific Palisades.
✚ C7 ✉ 118 Entrada Drive, Santa Monica ☎ 310/459-8596 🕐 Lunch, dinner daily 🚌 434

MICHAEL'S ($$$)
A California culinary pioneer, with an impressive contemporary art collection and lovely terrace.
✚ C8 ✉ 1147 3rd Street, Santa Monica ☎ 310/451-0843 🕐 Mon–Fri lunch, dinner; Sat dinner only 🚌 20, 33, SM2

ONE PICO ($$$)
The main dining room at Shutters, one of LA's loveliest hotels, offers seasonal California-Mediterranean food, which is paired with fabulous views of the Pacific.
✚ D8 ✉ One Pico Boulevard, Santa Monica ☎ 310/587-1717 🕐 Lunch, dinner daily 🚌 22, 33, SM8

RESTAURANT AT THE GETTY CENTER ($$)
Panoramic views, classic California cuisine and the classy ambience of this world-famous museum.
✚ D5 ✉ 1200 Getty Center Drive, West LA ☎ 310/440-6810 🕐 Tue–Sun lunch; Fri-Sat dinner 🚌 SM14

ROSE CAFÉ ($–$$)
Outdoor seating, tempting baked food and out-of-work actor/waiters, plus soothing ocean breezes.
✚ D8 ✉ 220 Rose Avenue, Venice Beach ☎ 310/399-0711 🚌 SM1, 8, 10

SADDLE PEAK LODGE ($$$)
Rustic hunting lodge hideaway in the Santa Monica Mountains. Excellent game dishes in season.
✚ Off map, west ✉ 419 Cold Canyon Road, Calabasas (San Fernando Valley) ☎ 818/222-3888 🕐 Wed–Sun lunch, dinner; Sun brunch

LA SERENATA GOURMET ($)
The Westside outpost of

A-MAIZING
Ground corn (*maíz* in Spanish) is a Mexican staple, and the chief ingredient of tortillas, the ubiquitous cornmeal pancakes that turn up in any number of guises on Mexican menus. Some of the most common varieties are soft, folded burritos, deep-fried enchiladas, crescent-shaped, deep-fried quesadillas filled with cheese and chilies (a useful vegetarian option) and crispy folded tacos (*taco* literally means "snack" in Mexico).

---

this Downtown favorite serves more upscale preparations, as well as its famous fish tacos, fresh tortillas and seafood.
✚ F7 ✉ 10924 W. Pico Boulevard, West LA ☎ 310/441-9667 🕐 Lunch, dinner daily; breakfast Sat–Sun 🚌 SM7

SIDEWALK CAFÉ ($)
Great people-watching from the beachfront terrace. Sandwiches, salads, tostadas and burgers.
✚ D9 ✉ 1401 Ocean Front Walk, Venice Beach ☎ 310/399-5547 🚌 33

VALENTINO ($$$)
Piero Selvaggi provides heavenly cuisine and an extensive wine list with white-glove service.
✚ E7 ✉ 3115 Pico Boulevard, Santa Monica ☎ 310/829-4313 🕐 Mon–Sat dinner, Fri lunch 🚌 SM7, 14

VERSAILLES ($)
A taste of Havana in Southern Cal serving large portions at good value.
✚ F7 ✉ 10319 Venice Boulevard, Palms ☎ 310/558-3168 🕐 Lunch, dinner daily 🚌 33

WORLD CAFÉ ($$)
Busy restaurant/bar with wood-fired pizzas, pastas and vegetarian dishes.
✚ D8 ✉ 2820 Main Street, Santa Monica ☎ 310/392-1661 🚌 33, SM1

A cultural hub northeast of downtown LA, Pasadena offers up world-class museums, sumptuous gardens, and every January, the famous Rose Bowl football game and the accompanying Tournament of Roses Parade.

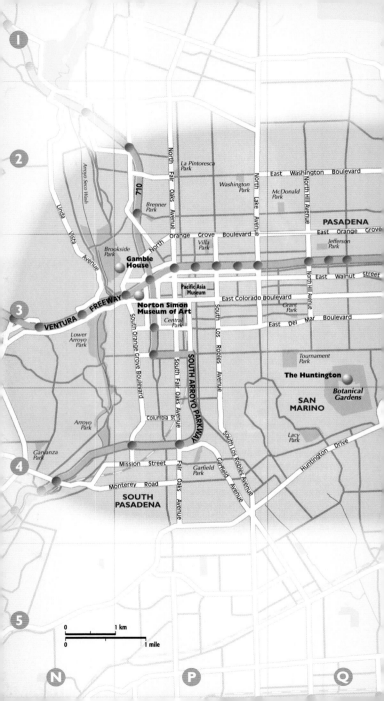

La Pintoresca
Park

East Washington Boulevard

Washington
Park

McDonald
Park

PASADENA

North Lake Avenue

North Hill Avenue

East Orange Grove

North Fair Oaks Avenue

710

Brenner
Park

North Orange Grove Boulevard

Villa
Park

Jefferson
Park

Brookside
Park

Gamble
House

East Walnut Street

North Hill Avenue

Linda Vista Avenue

Arroyo Seco Wash

Pacific Asia
Museum

East Colorado Boulevard

Norton Simon
Museum of Art

Grant
Park

East Del Mar Boulevard

VENTURA FREEWAY

Central
Park

South Orange Grove Boulevard

South Fair Oaks Avenue

SOUTH ARROYO PARKWAY

South Los Robles Avenue

Lower
Arroyo Park

Tournament
Park

The Huntington

Botanical
Gardens

SAN
MARINO

Arroyo
Park

Columbia Street

South Los Robles Avenue

Lacy
Park

Garvanza
Park

Mission Street

Fair Oaks Avenue

Garfield
Park

Garfield Avenue

Huntington Drive

Monterey Road

SOUTH
PASADENA

1 km

1 mile

N   P   Q

The Arboretum of LA County

TOP 25

Peacocks and palm trees are just two of the delights at the Arboretum

THE BASICS

www.arboretum.org
- ➕ S3
- ✉ 301 N. Baldwin Road, Arcadia (off I-210)
- ☎ 626/821-3222
- ⏱ Daily 9–5 (last ticket sales 4.30). Closed Christmas
- 🍴 Coffee shop
- 🚌 78, 79, 268
- ♿ Few
- 💵 Moderate
- ❓ Regular tram tours visit the extensive grounds

HIGHLIGHTS

- Queen Anne Cottage
- Santa Anita Railroad Depot
- Bird-watching
- Blooming jacaranda trees and Japanese irises

Set against the backdrop of the San Gabriel Mountains, these lovely gardens in a corner of the old Rancho Santa Anita offer year-round color and interest.

Mexican rancho Rancho Santa Anita was one of several ranches in the valley when Hugo Reid built his adobe house here in 1839. Furnished in simple pioneer style, it is one of three historic buildings in the grounds. The others are silver-mining millionaire E. J. "Lucky" Baldwin's fairy-tale 1881 Victorian cottage and the 1890 Santa Anita Railroad Depot.

From *Acacia* to *Ziziphus* The lush profusion of trees and plants (the arboretum is a favorite exotic movie location) includes exuberant jungle areas, towering palms, splashing waterfalls and quiet corners to enjoy the peace—as long as the raucous peacocks (introduced by Lucky Baldwin) are silent. Seek out the aquatic garden, the tropical greenhouse, the demonstration home gardens and the California landscape area, which shows the valley's natural state. There is much to see, so consider taking a tram tour to the farther reaches of the grounds (127 acres/51.4ha). The Arboretum also offers a variety of special events, from one-day classes to lectures to family treasure hunts. Check the website for dates and information.

More gardens in the area About 12 miles (19km) away is Descanso Gardens (1418 Descanso Drive, La Cañada Flintridge; tel 818/949-4200), 160 acres (65ha) of lovely landscaped property.

Gamble House was designed in 1908 and is now a National Historic Landmark

TOP 25

Gamble House

The Gamble House takes the utilitarian California Bungalow and turns it into an art form: Every impeccably handcrafted inch of the house is a masterpiece.

The California Bungalow The Gamble House, designed by the architect brothers Charles and Henry Greene for David and Mary Gamble (of Procter and Gamble fame), is the most complete and well-preserved example of a handful of luxurious wooden "bungalows" built in the first decade of the 20th century. The informal bungalow-style residence represented an appealing escape from Victorian stuffiness, and it was swiftly translated into southern California's architectural vernacular.

A symphony in wood However, it's far from a traditional bungalow. Greene and Greene's spreading two-floor design, with its Swiss- and Japanese-influenced lines, was planned in meticulous detail. The site was chosen to catch cool breezes from the Arroyo, and the arrangement of spacious verandas shaded by upper-floor sleeping porches and overhanging eaves keeps the house comfortably ventilated. Working largely in wood, the Greenes cloaked the exterior with shingles and created a rich, golden-timbered interior. Every fixture and fitting, from the dining room furniture to the irons in the fireplace, was custom-built, and many of the schemes were designed to complement Mary Gamble's favorite possessions such as Tiffany table lamps and opalescent Rockwood pottery. The excellent bookstore also sells self-guiding map tours around other Pasadena historic homes.

THE BASICS

www.gamblehouse.org

P3

4 Westmoreland Place, Pasadena (off N. Orange Grove)

626/793-3334

Thu–Sun 12–3. Closed national hols

401, transfer to 180, 267

None

Moderate

Admission by guided tour only; frequent departures

HIGHLIGHTS

● Front entrance: leaded glass by Emil Lange
● Main staircase
● Sitting room: carved reliefs of birds and plants
● Rugs from Greene and Greene designs
● Dining room furniture
● Tricks of the butler's pantry such as rollers for storing ironed tablecloths so that there were no creases
● Guest bedroom: maple furnishings inlaid with silver

91

The Huntington

- Ellesmere Chaucer and illuminated manuscripts
- *Pinkie*, Sir Thomas Lawrence
- Georgian Drawing Room, from Castle Hill, Devon
- *The Long Leg*, Hopper
- Japanese rock gardens
- Jungle garden, desert garden and lily ponds

TIP

- There is a free garden tour Tue–Fri 12–2, Sat–Sun 10.30–2.30 (depends on availability of volunteers).

Three elements—manuscripts, paintings and gardens—contribute to this famously rich and varied experience, and there hardly seems enough time to do each of them justice.

Collectors Henry E. Huntington (1850–1927) moved to LA in 1902 and made a second fortune organizing the city's rail system. When he retired, to devote himself to his library, he married his uncle's widow, Arabella, who shared his interest in art. Together they amassed 18th-century British portraits and French furnishings and decorative arts, bequeathing them for public benefit in 1919.

Manuscripts The Library building's extraordinary treasury of rare and precious manuscripts and books spans 800 years, from the famous 13th-

The beautiful gardens are one of the highlights of a visit to the Huntington; a Japanese-style tearoom in the grounds (bottom middle); the white mansion housing the Huntington Library (bottom right)

century Ellesmere Chaucer to handwritten drafts of novels and poems by, for example, William Blake, Walt Whitman and Jack London.

Fine art The 1910 Beaux Arts mansion displays the famous portrait collection, including Gainsborough's *Blue Boy*. Here too you will find ornate French furnishings and porcelain, and 18th-century European paintings added since Huntington's day. The Virginia Steele Scott Gallery houses American art, and furnishings from the Arts and Crafts team Greene and Greene (▷ 91).

Glorious gardens Huntington began work on the spectacular gardens in collaboration with William Hertrich in 1904. Today, there are about 15,000 types of plants and trees in 15 separate areas, including camellia woods and a rose garden.

THE BASICS

www.huntington.org

✚ Q3

✉ 1151 Oxford Road, San Marino (Pasadena)

☎ 626/405-2100

🕐 Sep–end May Tue–Fri 12–4.30, Sat–Sun 10.30–4.30; Jun–end Aug Tue–Sun 10.30–4.30. Closed major hols except Easter

🍴 Restaurant and tearoom

🚌 79, 379

♿ Good

✋ Moderate. Free first Thu of month

Norton Simon Museum of Art

Paintings inside the museum (left) and the sculpture garden (middle and right)

THE BASICS

www.nortonsimon.org

🔁 P3

✉ 411 W. Colorado Boulevard, Pasadena

☎ 626/449-6840

🕐 Wed–Mon 12–6 (Fri until 9)

🚍 401, transfer to 177, 180

♿ Good

💵 Moderate

HIGHLIGHTS

● *Branchini Madonna*, Giovanni di Paolo
● *Presumed Portrait of the Artist's Son, Titus*, Rembrandt
● *Burghers of Calais*, Rodin
● *The Stone Breakers*, Seurat
● *Exotic Landscape*, Rousseau
● *Flower Vendor*, Rivera
● *Odalisque with Tambourine*, Matisse
● *Woman with Book*, Picasso
● Degas Collection

Though the collections gathered here are not as well known as those in the Getty Center and LACMA, it is superior to both in many ways. If you only have time for one art stop, come here.

History The collections were originally founded as the Pasadena Art Institute in 1924. Under the direction of wealthy industrialist and collector Norton Simon (1907–93), the museum grew into a world-class collection of European Old Masters, Impressionist and Postimpressionist works, as well as Asian sculpture, arranged around a Frank Gehry-designed sculpture garden.

History of art The collections begin with jewel-like 14th-century Italian religious paintings and Renaissance art. The ravishing *Branchini Madonna* is just one of the highlights; the collection includes works by Filippino Lippi, Botticelli, Bellini and Cranach. From the 17th and 18th centuries there are Rembrandt portraits; Canaletto's minutely detailed Venetian scenes; soft, plump Tiepolo figures; and Rubens' oils on a heroic scale. The superb 19th- to 20th-century galleries show major works by Monet, Renoir, Cézanne and Van Gogh, and a fistful of color from Matisse, Kandinsky, Braque and Klee. The superb Degas Collection includes rare landscapes, enigmatic monotypes and an exceptional series of bronze dancers posthumously cast from wax models found in the artist's studio. The museum also possesses a rich collection of excellent Hindu and Buddhist sculpture from Nepal, India, Thailand and Cambodia.

Shopping

CANTERBURY RECORDS

This music shop has been in business 50-odd years and specializes in big band, jazz and classical music.

➕ P3 ✉ 805 E. Colorado Boulevard ☎ 626/792-7184
🚌 Pasadena, Rt. 10

MISSION STREET

This pretty, tree-shaded street has more than half a dozen antiques dealers, including furniture and collectables at Mission Antiques (No. 1018); Yoko

Japanese Antiques (No. 1011); and linen and bric-a-brac at Hodgson's Antiques (No. 1005).

➕ P4 ✉ Mission Street 🚇 Mission Street

OLD TOWN PASADENA

Bisected by Colorado Boulevard, this attractively restored enclave has appealing boutiques, galleries and eateries.

➕ P3 ✉ Colorado Boulevard (between Arroyo Parkway and Delacey Avenue)
🚌 Pasadena, Rt. 10

SOUTH LAKE AVENUE

Pasadena's major shopping area, with more than 100 stores.

➕ P3 ✉ Lake Avenue (between California and Colorado boulevards)
🚌 Pasadena, Rt. 10

VROMAN'S

The oldest bookstore in southern California, with a vast selection. There is also a branch selling stationery and gifts down the road at No. 667.

➕ P3 ✉ 695 E. Colorado Boulevard ☎ 626/449-5320
🚌 Pasadena, Rt. 10

Entertainment and Nightlife

BECKMAN AUDITORIUM

Host to the excellent Cal Tech performing arts season, which features theater, music, dance, comedy and lectures.

➕ Q3 ✉ 332 S. Michigan Avenue ☎ 626/395-4652
🚌 401

PASADENA CIVIC AUDITORIUM

Home of the Pasadena Symphony Orchestra, and a magnificent 1920s Moeller theater organ. Also various theater and dance events.

➕ P3 ✉ 300 E. Green Street ☎ 626/449-7360
🚌 401

ROSE BOWL

For more than 38 years, the Rose Bowl flea market (1001 Rose Bowl Drive in Pasadena) has attracted crowds looking for deals on everything from vintage toys to old books to Wedgwood jasperware. More than 2,200 vendors and approximately 20,000 buyers show up on the second Sunday of every month, rain or shine. Admission is $7 per person starting at 9am (for those who want to go earlier than 9am, admission is higher). The box office closes at 3pm, when vendors start packing up.

PASADENA POPS

Summer concerts in Descanso Gardens. Bring a picnic.

➕ M1 ✉ 1418 Descanso Drive, La Cañada
☎ 626/792–POPS 🚌 177

SANTA ANITA RACE TRACK

A track in the shadow of the San Gabriel Mountains. Thoroughbred horse-racing December 26 to late April, October, and November. Free viewing of morning workouts and weekend tram tours.

➕ S3 ✉ 285 W. Huntington Drive, Arcadia
☎ 626/574-7223 🚌 79, 188, 379

Restaurants

ARROYO CHOP HOUSE ($$$)

With its dark wood fittings, this well-established steak house is reminiscent of an old-fashioned club. The chef uses only prime beef, or you can have lamp chops or lobster, accompanied by your choice of simply prepared vegetables or salad.
🔲 P3 ✉ 536 S. Arroyo Parkway ☎ 626/577-7463 ⓘ Dinner daily Ⓜ Metro Gold Line 🚌 Pasadena, Rt. 51/52

BISTRO 45 ($$$)

"B45" serves tempting California-French cuisine in a restored art deco building. The wine list is particularly strong.
🔲 P3 ✉ 45 S. Mentor Avenue ☎ 626/795-2478 ⓘ Lunch and dinner Tue–Fri, dinner only Sat–Sun Ⓜ Metro Gold Line 🚌 Pasadena, Rt. 20

GORDON BIERSCH BREWERY ($$)

A Bay Area chain that expanded south, this spot has alfresco dining and people-watching, beers made on the premises and California cuisine.
🔲 P3 ✉ 41 Hugus Alley, Old Town Pasadena ☎ 626/449-0052 ⓘ Lunch, dinner daily Ⓜ Metro Gold Line 🚌 177

MI PIACE ($$)

This popular Italian serves the usual pasta dishes and crispy-crust New York-style pizzas with traditional toppings. The desserts are strong on chocolate.
🔲 P3 ✉ 25 E. Colorado Boulevard ☎ 626/795-3131 ⓘ Breakfast, lunch and dinner daily 🚌 Pasadena, Rt. 10

PARKWAY GRILL ($$$)

Here you will find cutting-edge California fare with Southwestern accents.

🔲 P3 ✉ 510 S. Arroyo Parkway ☎ 626/795-1001 ⓘ Lunch dinner daily Ⓜ Metro Gold Line 🚌 Pasadena, Rt. 51/52

THE RAYMOND ($$$)

Pretty, historic California bungalow with patios and a mixed menu.
🔲 P4 ✉ 1250 S. Fair Oaks Avenue ☎ 626/441-3136 ⓘ Lunch, dinner Tue–Sun 🚌 Pasadena, Rt. 51/52

SALADANG SONG ($)

Artfully presented Thai dishes include a vast assortment of noodle soups, as well as seafood, meat and vegetarian dishes.
🔲 P3 ✉ 383 S. Fair Oaks Avenue ☎ 626/793-5200 ⓘ Breakfast, lunch, dinner daily 🚌 Pasadena, Rt. 51/52

TWIN PALMS ($$–$$$)

Named for the huge trees that poke out of the dining room into the sky, this French country restaurant continues to impress. Live music on weekends.
🔲 P3 ✉ 101 W. Green Street ☎ 626/577-2567 ⓘ Lunch, dinner daily 🚌 Pasadena, Rt. 10

YUJEAN KANG'S ($$)

Chef Yujean Kang creates intriguing Chinese cuisine, with such dishes as "pictures in the snow."
🔲 P3 ✉ 67 North Raymond Avenue ☎ 626/585-0855 ⓘ Lunch, dinner daily 🚌 Pasadena, Rt. 10

Head south, north, or east from Los Angeles to discover a desert playground, the "American Riviera," the regal *Queen Mary*, and, of course, amusement parks, most notably Disneyland in Anaheim.

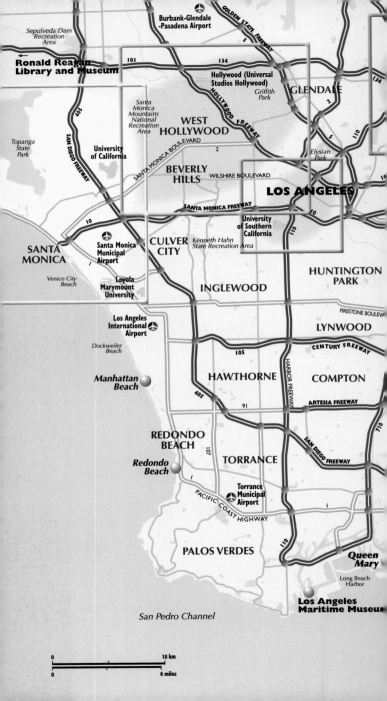

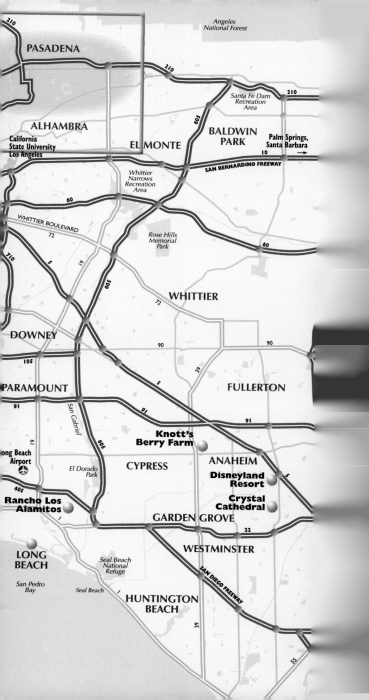

Disneyland Resort

© Disney Enterprises, Inc

© Disney Enterprises, Inc

HIGHLIGHTS

● Buzz Lightyear Astro
Blasters (Tomorrowland)
● Big Thunder Mountain
Railroad (Frontierland)
● California Screamin'
(California Adventure)
● Pirates of the Caribbean
(New Orleans Square)
● Splash Mountain (Critter
Country)
● Soarin' Over California
(California Adventure)

TIP

● Save money and time by
buying your tickets in
advance online.

**Since Disneyland opened its doors in
1955, Disney theme parks have become a
worldwide phenomenon. The 80-acre
(32ha) park, with its beguiling shows and
attractions, is still the daddy of them all.**

Magic Kingdom Brilliantly conceived and
operated like Swiss clockwork, the self-proclaimed
"Happiest Place on Earth" remains a perennial
winner. Disney's particular brand of fantasy
appeals across almost all age and cultural barriers.
The park is divided into eight individually themed
"lands." The gates open onto Main Street U.S.A., a
pastiche Victorian street lined with shops, which
leads to the hub of the park at Sleeping Beauty
Castle. From here you can explore the tropically
inspired Adventureland, home to the rattling roller
coaster ride Indiana Jones™ Adventure, or take a

World of Disney Store, Downtown Disney (left); Splash Mountain in Disneyland Park (middle); Block Party Bash parade (right); nighttime view of Disney's California Adventure Park (bottom)

© Disney Enterprises, Inc and Pixar

© Disney Enterprises, Inc

turn around Wild West-style Frontierland. Small children favor the simpler, cartoon-like rides in Fantasyland and Mickey's Toontown, while New Orleans Square is occupied by the spooky Haunted Mansion. Tomorrowland is a vision of the future.

Disney's California Adventure, an adjacent 55-acre (22ha) park, pays homage to the Golden State's unique character. Highlights, in six distinct areas, include a pier, forest and citrus grove.

Think ahead From July to early September, and in vacation periods, the park is very crowded and lines can be long. Weekends are especially busy. A free FASTPASS system is now in operation and saves your place in the line, giving a designated time frame in which to return and jump straight on the ride.

THE BASICS

www.disneyland.com

✚ Off map, south

✉ 1313 S. Harbor Boulevard (off I–5/Santa Ana Freeway), Anaheim

☎ 714/781-4565

🕐 Daily. Hours vary almost daily. Approximate hours peak season 8am–midnight; low season 10–8

🍴 Snack bars, cafés and restaurants

🚌 460

♿ Excellent

💲 Very expensive

Long Beach and the *Queen Mary*

Long Beach (left); The *Queen Mary* (right) held up to 1,957 passengers

THE BASICS

🗺 Off map, south

Long Beach Area Convention & Visitors Bureau
✉ One World Trade Center, Ocean Boulevard
☎ 562/436-3645
🕐 Mon–Fri 8–5
🚇 Pacific Avenue
🚌 60
🎟 Free

The *Queen Mary*
✉ Queen Mary Seaport, off I-710/Long Beach Freeway
☎ 562/435-3511
🕐 Daily 10–6
♿ Few
🎟 Expensive

Aquarium of the Pacific
✉ 100 Aquarium Way
☎ 562/590-3100
🕐 Daily 9–6
♿ Very good
🎟 Expensive

DID YOU KNOW?

● The *Queen Mary* was launched in 1934 and has more than 2,000 portholes.

An easy day trip south from central Los Angeles, Long Beach has plenty to offer—from the regal *Queen Mary* and jam-packed aquarium to water sports, shopping and gondola rides.

On the water A convenient first stop at the foot of the freeway, the *Queen Mary* finally came to rest here in 1967. What was once the largest liner afloat is now a hotel, but regular guided tours give access to the engine rooms, cabin suites and gorgeous art deco salons. Across the Queensway Bay Bridge (water taxi service available), the excellent Aquarium of the Pacific showcases more than 550 marine species from the northern Pacific to the tropics, including sharks, giant octopuses and California sea lions. East from here, Shoreline Drive skirts San Pedro Bay, passing the Long Beach Arena, encircled by the world's biggest mural, Plant Ocean, by the marine artist Wyland. Shoreline Village is popular for shopping and dining, with boat trips and views of the *Queen Mary*.

Downtown to Venice Island Pine Avenue, at the heart of Downtown Long Beach, bustles with shops and restaurants. Take Ocean Drive east to Belmont Shores, where concessionaires rent out water-sports equipment, and bicycles and skates for riding the beach path. Behind the beach, 2nd Street has shops and restaurants, and crosses on to Naples Island. This affluent residential neighborhood, crisscrossed with canals, was developed in the 1920s. Explore it on foot, or indulge in a relaxing ride with Gondola Getaway, tel 562/433-9595.

FARTHER AFIELD ★ TOP 25

Rancho Los Alamitos was home to pioneer ranching family the Bixbys

Rancho Los Alamitos

This historic ranch house brings a touch of the country to the heart of the city. The urban retreat grew up around what is believed to be the country's oldest domestic adobe.

Spanish land grant Built in 1806 and now tucked away behind the gates of an exclusive residential development not far from Long Beach, the ranch house was once master of all it surveyed. The original 28,500-acre (11,533ha) rancho was part of an enormous land grant allocated to a Spanish soldier, Manuel Nieto, in 1790. The Bixby family took possession in 1881, and the house remained in the family for almost a century until it was donated to the city of Long Beach in 1968.

A family home The Bixbys were one of southern California's most prominent pioneer ranching families, and Los Alamitos was the family home of Fred Bixby (1875–1952). From humble beginnings, the ranch house spread out on its hilltop site, and the views stretched across wheatfields to the ocean. During the 1920s and '30s, Fred's wife, Florence (1875–1961), set about developing the gardens, which are one of the highlights today. There is a distinctly Mexican-Mediterranean feel to the low whitewashed walls and shaded walkways. Tours of the house reveal that the original furnishings and family portraits are still in place. Five early 19th-century barns house a blacksmith's shop, tackroom and stables with Shire draft horses. Children will enjoy meeting and petting the sheep, goats, ducks, chickens, rabbits and doves.

THE BASICS

www.rancholosalamitos.com

✚ Off map, south
✉ 6400 Bixby Hill Road (take 7th Street east; left on Studebaker Road; left on Anaheim)
☎ 562/431-3541
🕐 Wed–Sun 1–5 (last tour at 4)
🚌 LBT 42
♿ Few
💲 Free
❓ Call for information about events and monthly Sunday afternoon education schedules (mostly free)

HIGHLIGHTS

● Rose garden, cacti collection and native Californian plantings
● Moreton Bay fig tree, planted in 1881

More to See

CRYSTAL CATHEDRAL

Close to Disneyland (▷ 100–101) is Phillip Johnson's mega structure with a glass ceiling and walls.

✚ Off map, south ✉ 12141 Lewis Street, Garden Grove ☎ 714/971-4013 ⏰ Tours Mon–Sat 9–3.30 ♿ None 💲 Inexpensive

KNOTT'S BERRY FARM

The nation's first theme park. Visit Camp Snoopy and the 1880s frontier Ghost Town, splash around in Soak City or ride some wild roller coasters.

✚ Off map, south ✉ 8039 Beach Boulevard, Buena Park ☎ 714/220-5200 ⏰ Call for schedules 🚌 460 💲 Very expensive

LOS ANGELES MARITIME MUSEUM

The largest maritime museum on the Pacific coast overlooks the busy Port of Los Angeles. There are dozens of beautifully crafted model ships, art, seafaring relics and real ships to visit.

✚ Off map, south ✉ Berth 84 (6th Street), San Pedro ☎ 310/548-7618 ⏰ Tue–Sat 10–5, Sun 12–5 🚌 447 💲 Inexpensive

MANHATTAN BEACH

Fashionable beach suburb with cafés along the seafront. Good swimming, surfing and games.

✚ Off map, south ✉ Manhattan Beach Boulevard (off Pacific Coast Highway) 🚌 439

REDONDO BEACH

Hotel-lined beach with good swimming and a heated lagoon for children. Fishing from the pier.

✚ Off map, south ✉ Off Pacific Coast Highway 🚌 439 🚉 Redondo Beach

RONALD REAGAN PRESIDENTIAL LIBRARY AND MUSEUM

After making a name for himself as an actor, Ronald Reagan went on to serve as governor of California before becoming the 40th president. Peruse his filmography, photographs, presidential gifts and papers; all on a 100-acre (41ha) site.

✚ Off map, north ✉ 40 Presidential Drive, Simi Valley ☎ 805/577-4000 ⏰ Daily 10–5 ♿ Good 💲 Moderate

Camp Snoopy at Knott's Berry Farm

Silver Bullet roller coaster at Knott's Berry Farm (opposite)

Manhattan Beach

★

Excursions

THE BASICS

Distance: 120 miles (192km)
Journey Time: 2–3 hours
❎ Palm Springs Regional Airport
🛈 2781 N. Palm Canyon Drive ☎ 760/770-8418
🕐 Daily 8–4

Knott's Soak City
✉ Gene Autry Trail and Highway 111, Cathedral City
☎ 760/327-0499
🕐 Opens for season in March

PALM SPRINGS

Famous for its many golf courses and hot nightlife, Palm Springs is "America's desert playground." Even if you don't play golf, there's plenty to do.

Palm Springs has a fine collection of Modernist buildings and great shopping. For families there's Knott's Soak City, with waterslides, "beaches" and a wave pool for surfing. If you want to explore the wilderness, try hiking in the Indian Canyons or take the Palm Springs Aerial Tramway up to the top of Mount San Jacinto (8,516ft/2,596m). The cars rotate on the way up to give you panoramic views. Joshua Tree National Park, 38 miles (62km) away, is a good place to explore the ecology of the Colorado and Mojave deserts.

THE BASICS

Distance: 92 miles (148km)
Journey Time: 1.5 hours
❎ Santa Barbara
🛈 1 Santa Barbara Street
☎ 805/966-9222
🕐 Mon–Fri 8.30–5

Santa Barbara Museum of Art
✉ 1130 State Street
☎ 805/963-4364
🕐 Tue–Sun 11–5

SANTA BARBARA

Santa Barbara, lying on the coast north of Los Angeles, bills itself as the "American Riviera." Its charming and compact Mediterranean-style downtown and waterfront parks have a lot to offer, from museums to beaches.

In 1925, Santa Barbara was destroyed by an earthquake and subsequently rebuilt in Spanish Mediterranean style. The resulting commercial district is a harmonious medley of adobe walls, rounded archways, glazed tilework and tile roofs. The Visitor Information Center can recommend walks that take you past the best buildings. The Museum of Art has an excellent collection, including works by Matisse and Chagall, while out of town the graceful Santa Barbara Mission overlooks the city and the ocean. The waterfront has pleasant parks and vast sandy beaches.

LA hotels are intertwined with celebrity lore: Liz Taylor spent six of her honeymoons at the Beverly Hills Hotel and John Belushi took a fatal overdose at Chateau Marmont. Visit a few of the famous ones, even if you don't rest your head there.

Introduction

LA has not only a wide variety of accommodations, as you would expect from a major city, but also a big choice in where to stay. The city is huge, and is not easily navigable by public transportation.

Location

This is a major consideration when choosing a hotel in a sprawling city like LA. Most hotels listed are on the main east–west transportation corridors between Downtown and the coast at Santa Monica. If your visit will last more than a few days, consider staying in a couple of different areas (Santa Monica and Hollywood, or Beverly Hills and Pasadena, for instance).

Hotels

Full-service hotels, concentrated in Downtown, the Westside and Beverly Hills, will include amenities such as fitness suites, indoor pools, laundry service, in-room internet access and valet parking, and this will be reflected in the price. In less fashionable areas, hotels tend to be smaller and less expensive. Most hotels do not include breakfast or parking in their rates, but may well allow children to share a room with their parents free of charge.

Other options

Motels are found mainly out of town directly on the highway; they often have swimming pools and cable TV. Your room opens directly to the outside so security may be an issue. There are hostels that charge as little as $10–$25 per night per person. Most have single-sex dorms, although some may have family rooms. Contact American Youth Hostels (www.hiayh.org). Bed-and-breakfasts are also popular (▷ panel, 110).

CAMPING

Most campgrounds in the area can be found in Malibu, which offers year-round camping for those who want to rough it. For reservations at Malibu Creek State Park, or other state parks in Southern California, call 800/444-7275. Note that sites are reserved months in advance.

Budget Hotels

BANANA BUNGALOW HOLLYWOOD HOSTEL

www.bananabungalow.com
This long-time favorite has rooms and dorms; friendly, international atmosphere; free airport pick-up, movie lounge, no curfew, laundry, kitchen, free parking.

H5 ✉ 7950 Melrose Avenue ☎ 877/977-5077 🍴 Restaurant 🚌 10, 11, 217

BAYSIDE HOTEL

www.baysidehotel.com
Great position across from the beach and one block from Main Street. 45 units.

D8 ✉ 2001 Ocean Avenue, Santa Monica ☎ 310/396-6000 or 800/525-4447 🍴 Restaurants nearby 🚌 4, 20, 22, 33, SM1, 7, 10

BEST WESTERN STOVALL'S INN

www.stovallshotels.com
Large resort hotel with 290 rooms, close to Disneyland, mobbed with kids. Free shuttles to Disneyland and Anaheim, kids' menu, pool.

Off map, south ✉ 1110 W. Katella Avenue, Anaheim ☎ 714/778-1880 or 800/854-8177 🍴 Restaurants nearby 🚌 460

BEVERLY LAUREL MOTOR HOTEL

Terrific location near Beverly Center, Farmer's Market, Melrose Avenue and Museum Row. Kitchens available. 52 rooms.

G6 ✉ 8018 Beverly Boulevard, Midtown ☎ 323/651-2441; fax 323/651-2441 🚌 14, 316

DESERT INN & SUITES

www.anaheimdesertinn.com
Well-equipped rooms (145) and good facilities close to Disneyland. Pool.

Off map, south ✉ 1600 S. Harbor Boulevard, Anaheim ☎ 714/772-5050 or 800/433-5270 🍴 Restaurants nearby, breakfast included 🚌 460

FARMER'S DAUGHTER

www.farmersdaughterhotel.com
Across the street from the Farmers Market, this friendly family-owned

budget option was recently renovated. There are 66 rooms, a pool, and an on-site restaurant called Tart.

H6 ✉ 115 S. Fairfax Avenue ☎ 323/937-3930 or 800/334-1658 🚌 14, 16, 217

HOLIDAY INN HOLLYWOOD WALK OF FAME

www.holidayinn.com
160 modern rooms. Facilities include a heated swimming pool, spa and fitness center.

H5 ✉ 2005 N. Highland Avenue ☎ 323/876-8600 or 800/972-2576 🍴 Café, bar Ⓜ Metro Red Line 🚌 212, 217

HOSTELLING INTERNATIONAL

Good-size hostel (260 beds) close to the Santa Monica Pier. Good facilities, with a courtyard, laundry, library, tours, activities. Some private rooms are available.

D8 ✉ 1436 2nd Street, Santa Monica ☎ 310/393-9913 🚌 20, 22, 33, SM8

THE INN AT VENICE BEACH

www.innatvenicebeach.com
A modern motel close to the Venice Boardwalk, with a European feel and free Continental breakfast. There are 43 units.

E9 ✉ 327 Washington Boulevard, Venice ☎ 310/821-2557 or 800/828-0688 🍴 Restaurants nearby 🚌 33, SM2, 3

Mid-Range Hotels

WHERE TO STAY MID-RANGE HOTELS

PRICES

Expect to pay between $150 and $300 per night for a mid-range hotel.

THE BELAMAR HOTEL

Near LAX in Manhattan Beach, this hotel has 127 guest rooms and suites, though none with ocean views. Rooms have flat-screen TVs and sumptuous linens; Chihuahua pictures are scattered throughout the property.
🔲 Off map, south ✉ 3501 Sepulveda Boulevard, Manhattan Beach
🍴 Restaurant ☎ 310/750-0300

BEST WESTERN OCEAN VIEW HOTEL

www.bestwestern.com
A great choice if you want an affordable beach location, the Ocean View is just across from Santa Monica pier. All 65 rooms are clean and modern with internet access, and many have balconies and ocean views.
🔲 D8 ✉ 1447 Ocean Avenue, Santa Monica
☎ 310/458-4888 or 800/452-4888 🍴 Breakfast included
🚌 7, 8

BEST WESTERN SUNSET PLAZA HOTEL

www.bestwestern.com
This may not be the city's most glamorous hotel, but the location right on Sunset Strip is hard to beat. The 100 rooms are spacious and some have

kitchens. The public areas were renovated in 2006.
🔲 G5 ✉ 8400 Sunset Boulevard ☎ 323/654-0750 or 800/421-3652 🍴 Breakfast included 🚌 2, 302

CARLYLE INN

Delightful 32-room hotel with spa, fitness center, free local shuttle and complimentary breakfast buffet. No pool.
🔲 G6 ✉ 1119 S. Robertson Boulevard, West LA
☎ 310/275-4445 or 800/322-7595 🚌 220

CHANNEL ROAD INN BED AND BREAKFAST

www.channelroadinn.com
An original 1910 Colonial Revival house in Santa Monica Canyon, crammed with period antiques. The 14 rooms are individually decorated and have private baths.

BED-AND-BREAKFAST

Bed-and-breakfasts and private home stays are popular alternatives to hotels. The California Association of Bed & Breakfast Inns (CABBI) (☎ 831/462-9191; www.cabbi.com) is a non-profit organization that represents close to 350 bed-and-breakfasts and inns throughout California. All CABBI establishments must meet quality standards, such as exemplary housekeeping, operate full-time and include breakfast in the price of the room.

Bicycles, library and a hot tub are available, and tea and cookies are laid on each afternoon, with wine and cheese in the evenings.
🔲 C7 ✉ 219 W. Channel Road ☎ 310/459-1920 🚌 9

EMBASSY HOTEL APARTMENTS

Near the Third Street Promenade and the ocean, these Mediterranean-style apartments, built in 1927, offer numerous suites with kitchen and separate bedroom. Single rooms are also available.
🔲 C7 ✉ 1001 Third Street, Santa Monica ☎ 310/394-1279 🚌 4, 20, 22, SM1, 2, 3, 7, 8, 9, 10

FIGUEROA HOTEL

www.figueroahotel.com
Useful central business hotel. Also used as a convention center.
🔲 L6 ✉ 939 S. Figueroa Street ☎ 213/627-8971 or 800/421-9092 🍴 Restaurant
🚌 DASH C, F

FOUR POINTS HOTEL

A comfortable airport bargain with a 24-hour fitness room. 573 rooms.
🔲 Off map, south ✉ 9750 Airport Boulevard, LAX
☎ 310/645-4600 or 800/529-4683 🍴 Restaurant

HILTON CHECKERS HOTEL

www.hiltoncheckers.com
This elegant hotel is a good option for visitors searching for 4-star luxury in Downtown. There's a

rooftop swimming pool, spa and good restaurant. 🏠 L6 ✉ 535 S. Grand Avenue ☎ 213/624-0000 🚍 DASH B, C

HOLIDAY INN & SUITES ANAHEIM
www.hianaheim.com
Old West-theme hotel; 255 rooms, games room, babysitting, free shuttle to nearby Disneyland.
🏠 Off map, south ✉ 1240 S. Walnut Street, Anaheim ☎ 714/535-0300 or 800/824-5459 🍽 Restaurants 🚍 460

HOLLYWOOD ROOSEVELT HOTEL
www.hollywoodroosevelt.com
Refurbished Hollywood legend (▷ 36) with some poolside cabana rooms among the 305 units.
🏠 H5 ✉ 7000 Hollywood Boulevard, Hollywood ☎ 323/466-7000 or 800/950-7667 🍽 Good restaurant 🚍 212, 217

MALIBU COUNTRY INN
Intimate New England romance with just 16 rooms. All have private patios.
🏠 Off map, west ✉ 6506 Westward Beach Road, Malibu ☎ 310/457-9622 or 800/386-6787 🍽 Continental breakfast included 🚍 434

MILLENNIUM BILTMORE HOTEL LOS ANGELES
www.millenniumhotels.com
A Historical Cultural Landmark, the Biltmore opened in 1923 and has many historical associations. It was once home to the Academy Awards and birthplace of the Oscar, and was the headquarters for JFK's 1960 presidential campaign. The rooms themselves may be unexciting, but the grandeur of the public areas and the thoughtful service compensate for this.
🏠 L6 ✉ 506 S. Grand Avenue ☎ 213/624-1011 or 800/245-8673 🍽 Restaurant 🚍 DASH B, C

NEW OTANI HOTEL
www.newotani.com
This contemporary high-rise in Little Tokyo is close to the Convention Center, the Musi Center and Union Station. The rooms are plain but perfectly comfortable, and there's a restful Japanese garden and spa.
🏠 L6 ✉ 120 S. Los Angeles Street ☎ 213/629-1200 🍽 Restaurant 🚍 DASH A, D

THE STANDARD
A former retirement home, with 139 units, now bustles with young guests and nightly DJ action.
🏠 G5 ✉ 8300 Sunset Boulevard, West Hollywood ☎ 323/650-9090 🍽 24-hour restaurant, bars 🚍 2, 302

UNIVERSAL CITY HILTON & TOWERS
Universal Studios packages, good family and business facilities. 483 units.
🏠 H3 ✉ 555 Universal Hollywood Drive, Universal City ☎ 818/506-2500 or 800/HILTONS 🍽 Restaurant 🚍 422, 433

VALADON HOTEL
www.valadonhotel.com
Classy hotel in the residential district of Melrose Place, equidistant from Beverly Hills and Hollywood. It has 80 luxurious units with refrigerators and fireplaces, and a rooftop garden swimming pool.
🏠 G5 ✉ 8822 Cynthia Street ☎ 310/854-1114 or 800/835-7997 🍽 Restaurants nearby 🚍 2, 10, 11

MAGIC ACT
When traveling with children, the Magic Castle Hotel (✉ 7025 Franklin Avenue, Hollywood ☎ 800/741-4915), a 40-unit option in Hollywood, has a unique offering: professional tricksters. Adults have access to the private Magic Castle Club in the evenings, while families can see the magic show at brunch on weekends. Rooms and suites come equipped with full kitchens; Continental breakfast is included.

Luxury Hotels

AVALON HOTEL

www.avalonbeverlyhills.com
Private cabanas and the restaurant are clustered around the central pool terrace at this ultrastylish hideaway. The comfortable rooms are stylishly decorated in neutral hues.
🔼 F6 ✉ 9400 W. Olympic Boulevard, Beverly Hills
☎ 310/277-5221 or 800/670-6183 🍴 7, 28

BEVERLY HILLS HOTEL

www.beverlyhillshotel.com
Legendary pink palace on a 12-acre (5ha) landscaped and palm-fringed site. Hollywood feel in 204 rooms.
🔼 F5 ✉ 9641 Sunset Boulevard, Beverly Hills
☎ 310/276-2251 or 800/283-8885 🍴 Two restaurants, coffee shop, poolside café
🍴 2, 3

BEVERLY WILSHIRE

www.fourseasons.com
Sumptuous European-style, 395-room hotel.
🔼 F6 ✉ 9500 Wilshire Boulevard, Beverly Hills
☎ 310/275-5200 or 800/819-5053 🍴 Excellent restaurant, The Dining Room 🍴 20, 21, 220

CHATEAU MARMONT

www.chateaumarmont.com
Castle-style 1927 favorite of Gable, Lombard, Harlow et al. John Belushi died here. 63 units.
🔼 G5 ✉ 8221 Sunset Boulevard, West Hollywood
☎ 323/656-1010 or 800/242-8328 🍴 Dining room with fine wine cellar 🍴 2, 3

HOTEL BEL-AIR

www.hotelbelair.com
LA's most romantic hotel, with 91 units tucked away in a wooded canyon.
🔼 E5 ✉ 701 Stone Canyon Road, Bel-Air ☎ 310/472-1211 or 800/648-4097 🍴 Restaurant

LOS ANGELES MARRIOTT DOWNTOWN

www.losangelesmarriottdowntown.com
Fine Downtown hotel with 400 guest rooms and 69 suites, wall-to-wall windows and superb city views.
🔼 L6 ✉ 333 S. Figueroa Street ☎ 213/617-1133 or 800/228-9290 🍴 Very good restaurant and grill
🍴 DASH A

MONDRIAN

www.mondrianhotel.com
238 large rooms with scented candles, CDs, orchids and city views.
🔼 G5 ✉ 8440 Sunset Boulevard ☎ 323/650-8999 or 800/697-1791
🍴 Restaurant, Sky Bar (▷ 45) 🍴 2, 3

PENINSULA BEVERLY HILLS

www.beverlyhills.peninsula.com
Ultrachic hideaway for celebrities, with discreet and personalized service. 196 splendid rooms.
🔼 F6 ✉ 9882 Little Santa Monica Boulevard, Beverly Hills ☎ 310/551-2888 or 800/462-7899 🍴 Belvedere Restaurant (▷ 46) 🍴 21, 27, 316

RITZ-CARLTON HUNTINGTON

www.ritzcarlton.com
Beautifully restored 1907 hotel; 392 units, luxurious facilities, stunning gardens.
🔼 P4 ✉ 1401 S. Oak Knoll, Pasadena ☎ 626/568-3900 or 800/241-3333 🍴 Famous grill room

SHUTTERS ON THE BEACH

www.shuttersonthebeach.com
198 lovely New England-style rooms on the beach.
🔼 D8 ✉ One Pico Boulevard, Santa Monica ☎ 310/458-0030 or 800/334-9000 🍴 Very good restaurant, One Pico (▷ 86)
🍴 22, 33, SM8

With an average of 329 days of sunshine per year, LA welcomes a steady stream of visitors year-round. The city's size and perennial traffic, however, require a bit of patience, so it's wise to plan ahead.

Planning Ahead

When to Go

Los Angeles is mild and temperate, with sunshine and fair weather pretty much guaranteed from May to October. Humidity ranges from 65 to 77 percent. Spring, early summer and early fall are the best times to visit; crowds aren't too big and the weather should be perfect. Beware of overcast skies in June, especially at the coast—Angelenos call this June gloom.

TIME
Los Angeles is on Pacific Standard Time (US West Coast); 3 hours behind New York, 8 hours behind the UK.

AVERAGE DAILY MAXIMUM TEMPERATURES

JAN	FEB	MAR	APR	MAY	JUN	JUL	AUG	SEP	OCT	NOV	DEC
65°F	66°F	69°F	71°F	74°F	77°F	83°F	83°F	82°F	77°F	73°F	68°F
18°C	19°C	21°C	22°C	23°C	25°C	28°C	28°C	28°C	25°C	23°C	20°C

Spring (mid-March to late June) is usually dry and comfortable.

Summer (late-June to mid-September) is perfect beach and theme-park weather. Late summer can be smoggy, though humidity is usually low.

Fall (mid-September to November) is fair to warm. Days are gorgeous, nights crisp.

Winter (December to mid-March) brings warm days interspersed with cool and even freezing nights. Sweaters and jackets are usually neccessary after dark.

WHAT'S ON

January *Rose Parade*: Pasadena's New Year's Day spectacular accompanying the Rose Bowl football game.

February *Chinese New Year*: The Golden Dragon Parade winds through Chinatown.

Academy Awards: Celebrities hit Hollywood.

March *LA Marathon and Bike Tour*.

April *Thai New Year*: Focuses on the magnificent Wat Thai temple in North Hollywood.

May *Cinco de Mayo*: Mexico's independence day, liveliest on Olvera Street.

June *Playboy Jazz Festival*: Hollywood Bowl.

Gay and Lesbian Pride Celebration: West Hollywood Park.

July *Lotus Festival*: One of the largest Lotus beds outside China is at Echo Park Lake.

July–September *Hollywood Bowl Summer Festival*: Evening open-air concerts.

August *Nisei Week*: Japanese-American cultural heritage event.

September *Los Angeles Birthday Celebrations*: Celebrates the founding of the city.

LA County Fair: LA County Fairplex Fairgrounds, Pomona

October *City of the Angels Film Festival*: The Director's Guild of America hosts.

November *Dia de los Muertos*: Olvera Street celebrates the Day of the Dead.

Doo Dah Parade: Pasadena's Rose Parade spoof.

December *Hollywood Christmas Parade*: With celebrity guests.

Griffith Park Lighting Festival: Month-long spectacular light display.

Los Posadas: Mary and Joseph's search for shelter is commemorated.

Los Angeles Online

www.lacvb.com
The Los Angeles Convention and Visitor's Bureau covers cultural attractions, suggested itineraries, city statistics and general travel information. The site also has useful links.

www.losangeles.citysearch.com
You'll get loads of interesting information; the top celebrity hangouts, chic shops, new movies, hot pubs, and a range of picks from the best spa to the tastiest burrito.

www.calendarlive.com
This weekly section in the *Los Angeles Times* gives a comprehensive overview of current films, theater, exhibits, lectures, concerts, sports and other entertainment happenings in and around the city. Reviewers also give input.

www.latimes.com
The daily *Los Angeles Times* has national and local news, and sections devoted to entertainment, food, sports, politics, health, southern California living, religion and real estate.

www.lamag.com
The online version of the slick monthly *Los Angeles Magazine* is a great guide to restaurants, museums, nightclubs, outdoor events, concerts, flea markets and coffee houses.

www.losangeles.com
Loads of information about the city including music, dining, arts, shopping, history and visitor information sources. You can make hotel and car rental reservations online.

www.ci.la.ca.us
The official website of the City of Los Angeles provides tourist and recreational information as well as a detailed introduction to the city.

www.lawa.org
The official website for Los Angeles World Airports.

USEFUL TRAVEL SITES

www.theAA.com
A great resource for the essentials, ranging from destination information to travel insurance policies. There is also a UK facility for ordering travel guides and maps online.

www.fodors.com
A complete travel-planning site. You can research prices and weather; book air tickets, cars and rooms; ask questions (and get answers) from fellow travelers; and find links to other sites.

CYBERCAFÉS

FedEx Kinko's
Branches throughout the LA area offer internet access and business services. Prices vary, but internet access is about 25¢ per minute.
➕ L5 ✉ 835 Wilshire Blvd.
☎ 213/892-1700
◉ Mon–Thu 6am–11pm, Fri 6am–8pm, Sat–Sun 8–8

➕ J5 ✉ 1440 Vine St.
☎ 323/871-1300 ◉ Mon 7am–midnight, Tue–Thu 24 hours, Fri midnight–10pm, Sat–Sun 9am–8pm

➕ G5 ✉ 8471 Beverly Blvd.
☎ 323/782-6905
◉ Mon–Fri 7am–11pm, Sat–Sun 9am–8pm

NEED TO KNOW PLANNING AHEAD

Getting There

ENTRY REQUIREMENTS

Visitors to the US must show a full passport, valid for at least six months. Most UK citizens and visitors from other countries belonging to the Visa Waiver Program can enter without a visa, but you must have a return or onward ticket. However, regulations can change so check before you travel. Check with the US Embassy ☎ 020 7499 9000; www.usembassy.org.uk

CUSTOMS

● Visitors from outside the US, aged 21 or over, may import duty-free: 200 cigarettes or 50 non-Cuban cigars, or 4.4lb (2kg) of tobacco; 2 pints (1L) of liquor; and gifts up to $100 in value.

● Restricted import items include meat, seeds, plants and fruit.

● Some medication bought over the counter abroad may be prescription-only in the US and may be confiscated. Bring a doctor's certificate for essential medication.

AIRPORTS

Los Angeles International Airport (LAX) lies 17 miles (27km) southwest of Downtown. It is served by all major domestic carriers and many international airlines. The flight from London takes around 10 hours; from New York 6 hours.

FROM LOS ANGELES INTERNATIONAL AIRPORT

For airport information ☎ 310/646-5252. Car rental companies provide free shuttles to their parking lots from the ground transportation island outside the lower level baggage claim areas.

To drive into Downtown from Airport Boulevard, take I-405 through West Los Angeles. Possibly quicker is to take La Tijera Boulevard, then go north on La Cienega Boulevard into West LA. La Cienega intersects both Wilshire and Olympic boulevards, which run east through Downtown.

Door-to-door 24-hour shuttle bus services to all areas of the city, such as SuperShuttle (☎ 800/554-3146), also depart from the ground transportation island. The journey to Downtown takes around 30–60 minutes, depending on traffic, and costs $12–$16. The Metro Airport Service provides shuttle buses between all eight terminals (Shuttle A), and the remote parking lots (Shuttle B and Shuttle C). Shuttle C serves the terminal for bus connections to the city ($1.85–$3.35).

A cab to Downtown or Hollywood costs $35–$45 and takes 30–60 minutes.

LAX BY DESIGN
The control tower at the Los Angeles International Airport was created by local architect Kate Diamond, whose 1995 design evokes a stylized palm tree. It makes a fine counterpoint to the nearby Theme Building, the spidery structure that has long been the symbol of LAX and contains the space-fantasy restaurant called Encounter.

ARRIVING BY AIR: OUTSIDE LOS ANGELES
If you are flying in from other states or cities in the US, you may arrive at one of the region's many smaller airports, which include Bob Hope Airport, formerly Burbank Airport (☎ 818/840-8840) in Burbank; John Wayne Airport (☎ 949/252-5200) in Santa Ana; Long Beach Municipal Airport (☎ 562/570-2600); or Ontario International Airport in Ontario, convenient only if you are headed first to the desert.

ARRIVING BY BUS
LA's main Greyhound/Trailways terminal is Downtown ✉ 1716 E. 7th Street. There are also terminals in Anaheim, Hollywood, Pasadena and Santa Monica. For more information ☎ 800/231-2222.

ARRIVING BY TRAIN
Visitors and commuters arrive at Union Station ✉ 800 N. Alameda Street, just north of Downtown, on the Metro Red Line and DASH shuttle bus routes. For Amtrak information ☎ 800/872-7245.

EXTRA INFO
DASH routes
www.ladottransit.com/dash/routes/downtown/downtown.html
Metro/bus
www.metro.net/images/System_Map.pdf

INSURANCE
● Domestic travelers should check their policies and ensure they are covered against loss and theft as well as medical emergencies.
● For non-US citizens, it is vital that travel insurance covers medical expenses in addition to accidents, trip cancellation, baggage loss and theft. Check the policy covers any continuing treatment for a chronic condition.

VISITORS WITH A DISABILITY
Visitors with disabilities should have no trouble navigating LA, one of the world's leaders in assuring an accessible environment. All public buildings are wheelchair accessible. In addition, almost every attraction, hotel and restaurant offers access. Most street corners have sloped curbs, and city buses are fitted with automatic wheelchair lifts, handgrips and designated seating areas. For more information contact ✉ Mobility International USA, 132 E. Broadway, Suite 343, Eugene, Oregon ☎ 541/343-1284

NEED TO KNOW   GETTING THERE

Getting Around

THE METRO (MTA)

www.mta.net
☎ 1/800-COMMUTE

The Los Angeles County Metropolitan Transit Authority (MTA) runs the Metro buses and rail lines and provides the most extensive coverage of the city, although many lines have a reduced evening and weekend service.

● Buses run roughly every 15 minutes, with a reduced service at night.

● The Metro system has 200 Metro Bus lines and five Metro Rail lines, covering about 60 miles (97km), but they are only of limited use when trying to get from one part of the city to another.

● A single journey by bus or rail is $1.25, while the Metro Day Pass, which gives unlimited use of all Metro bus and rail lines for a day, costs $3. You can buy it at any Metro station or on board any Metro bus.

● A single ticket is only valid on one line. If you change lines, you must buy another ticket.

● There is a small additional fee of 25c for transferring to a municipal bus, referred to as Metro to Muni Transfer.

● There are no gates to pass through or conductors to collect tickets, but MTA does carry out random ticket inspections.

BUSES

● Buses operated by the Los Angeles County Metropolitan Transit Authority (MTA or Metro; www.mta.net) provide the most extensive coverage of the city, but many lines have a reduced evening and weekend service.

● The DASH Downtown shuttle bus service (operated by Los Angeles Department of Transportation; www.ladottransit.com) operates within the Downtown Financial District extending out to Exposition Park in the south and north to Chinatown via Union Station and El Pueblo (☎ 808-2273 [same number for area codes 213, 310, 323, 818] ⏰ Every 5–15 minutes, Mon–Fri 6.30–6.30; limited weekend service 🖐 25¢).

● The MTA bus services most useful to visitors are the main east–west routes Downtown to Santa Monica, and north–south to the South Bay.

● Have correct change ready for the machine on boarding. Fares are based on the number of zones traveled and certain express services cost more. Evening services (between 9pm–5am) cost just 75¢.

METRO

● The Red Line subway extends from Union Station across Downtown and west on Wilshire Boulevard all the way to North Hollywood.

● The Blue Line runs above ground from downtown to Long Beach, which takes about 45 minutes.

● The Gold Line goes from Union Station northeast to Pasadena.

● The Green Line goes from Norwalk, in the southeast, to Redondo Beach, in the southwest. It's the line that passes closest to the airport but is otherwise of little interest to tourists.

● The Purple Line shares six stations with the Red Line and continues to mid-Wilshire.

● Each of the 50 subway stations is adorned with interesting original art.

TAXIS

● It is virtually impossible to hail a cab in the street, except possibly Downtown. Hotels and transport terminals are good places to find a cab, and restaurants will order one for you at the end of your evening.
● Useful taxi firms are:
Checker Cab ☎ 213/482-3456
Independent Cab ☎ 213/385-8294
LA Taxi ☎ 310/859-0111

DRIVING

● LA is a sprawling city not that well served by public transportation, so it's a good idea to rent a car at the airport to get around. However, as everyone else is also driving, traffic snarls are an almost constant hazard. These are useful routes from LAX:
● To reach Marina del Rey, Venice, Santa Monica and Malibu, follow the signs to Sepulveda Boulevard north, then leave Sepulveda to take Lincoln Boulevard (here serving as Highway 1) to head north.
● For the Westside and Beverly Hills, follow the signs to Century Freeway (105) or take Century Boulevard east to the San Diego Freeway (405). Head north on 405 till you cross Santa Monica Freeway (10), then exit on Santa Monica, Wilshire or Sunset boulevards.
● For Hollywood, take 105 east to 405 north to 10 east to 110 north (toward Pasadena), then take the Hollywood Freeway (101) toward Hollywood. Alternatively, take 405 north to 10 east and get off at La Brea, La Cienega or Fairfax, and head north toward West Hollywood and the Hollywood Hills.
● For Downtown, take Century Freeway (105) east to Harbor Freeway (110) north toward Pasadena to reach Downtown exits.
● To reach Pasadena, follow the directions for Downtown above, but continue north on 110 (the name changes to Pasadena Freeway once you're north of LA).
● Seatbelts are required and children under 7 must be secured in a safety or booster seat.

RULES OF THE ROAD

● It is legal to turn right on a red light unless otherwise posted.
● Pedestrians have right of way at crosswalks.
● At four-way crossings without traffic lights, the law decrees that cars cross in order of arrival at the intersection; if two cars arrive simultaneously, the car to the right has priority. In reality, it is he who dares that wins.
● Freeway car pool lanes can be used by any car carrying the requisite number of passengers (generally two or three), indicated by signs posted on the freeway.
● Unless otherwise posted, the speed limit is 55 or 65mph (88 or 104kph) on urban freeways, 35mph (56kph) on major thoroughfares, 25mph (40kph) on residental and other streets.

GUIDED TOURS IN LA

Los Angeles Conservancy
☎ 213/623-2489. Themed walking tours.
Hollywood Fantasy Tours
☎ 323/469-8184. The classic star tour (by bus).
Casablanca Tours
☎ 323/461-0156. Showbiz tours.
American Limousines
☎ 310/829-1066
Gondola Getaway
☎ 562/433-9595

Essential Facts

MONEY

The unit of currency is the dollar (=100 cents). Notes (bills) come in denominations of $1, $5, $10, $20, $50 and $100; coins come in 25¢ (a quarter), 10¢ (a dime), 5¢ (a nickel) and 1¢ (a penny).

5 dollars

10 dollars

50 dollars

100 dollars

CONSULATES

● Australia ✉ Century Plaza Towers, 19th Floor, 2049 Century Park East ☎ 310/229-4800
● Denmark ✉ 18077 Wilshire Boulevard ☎ 310/481-0391
● Germany ✉ 6222 Wilshire Boulevard ☎ 323/930-2703
● Netherlands ✉ 11766 Wilshire Boulevard 310/268-1598
● New Zealand ✉ 2425 Olympic Boulevard ☎ 310/566-6555
● Sweden ✉ 10940 Wilshire Boulevard, Suite 700 ☎ 310/445-4008
● UK ✉ Suite 1200, 11766 Wilshire Boulevard ☎ 310/481-0031

ETIQUETTE

● LA dress is casual. Men rarely don jacket or tie to dine in even the smartest restaurants.
● Smoking is illegal in all public buildings, and is now banned in bars and restaurants as well. It is permitted in outdoor seating areas of restaurants, though do not expect your neighbors to be friendly about it. There are designated smoking rooms in most hotels.
● Tipping: 15–20 percent is expected by waiters; 15 percent for cab drivers; $1–$2 per bag for porters; $1 per item for cloakroom attendants; 15–20 percent for hairdressers; and $1–$2 is usual for valet parking.

LIQUOR LAWS

● Bars can open at any time between 6am and 2am, though most open around 11am and close around midnight (later on Friday and Saturday). Licensed restaurants can serve liquor throughout their hours of business except between 2am and 6am. To buy or consume liquor in California, you must be 21 or older. Expect to be asked for ID.

LOST AND FOUND

● LA International Airport: Contact your airline and ask for its lost-and-found department.

- Airport police ☎ 310/417–0440
- MTA (Metrobuses and Metrolink) for lost property ☎ 323/937–8920
- Otherwise call the relevant police precinct. The addresses and phone numbers for the police are listed in the local telephone book.

EMERGENCY NUMBER

Fire, police, or ambulance
☎ 911 (no money required)

MAIL AND TELEPHONES

- Post offices are generally open Mon–Fri 8.30 or 9am to 6pm; Sat until 1 or 2pm.
- Local calls cost 35¢.
- LA has a number of local telephone codes. Some calls within the LA area require more than a 35¢ deposit. Dial the number and a recorded operator message gives the minimum deposit.
- The area code for Downtown Los Angeles is 213; other useful area codes include 323 (the area immediately surrounding Downtown and Hollywood); 310 (Beverly Hills, the Westside, Santa Monica); 562 (Long Beach and other South Bay areas); 626 (Pasadena); 818 (San Fernando Valley).
- Many businesses have free phone numbers, prefixed 800 or 888. First dial "1" (i.e. "1–800").
- To call the US from the UK dial 001. To call the UK from the US dial 011 44, then drop the first "0" from the area code.

MEDICAL TREATMENT

- Many hotels can arrange for referrals to a local doctor or dentist. Or look under "Physicians and Surgeons" or "Dentists" in the Yellow Pages.
- Most city hospitals accept emergency cases. Those with well-equipped 24-hour emergency rooms include:
Cedars-Sinai Medical Center ✉ 8700 Beverly Boulevard, West Hollywood ☎ 310/423-8780 and Good Samaritan Hospital ✉ 1225 Wilshire Boulevard, Downtown ☎ 213/977-2121

NEED TO KNOW ESSENTIAL FACTS

Essential Facts

MEDICINES

● Pharmacies are plentiful; look in the *Yellow Pages*.
● Visitors from outside the US using medication regularly will find that although many familiar drugs are available (probably under unfamiliar names), it is preferable to bring a supply.
● If you intend to buy prescription drugs in the US, bring a note from your doctor.

MONEY MATTERS

● Nearly all banks have ATMs.
● Credit cards, a secure alternative to cash, are widely accepted.
● US dollar traveler's checks function like cash in all but small shops; $20 and $50 denominations are most useful.
● An 8.25 percent sales tax is added to all retail prices.

NEWSPAPERS AND MAGAZINES

● LA's English-language daily newspapers are the *Los Angeles Times* (local and international news) and the *Los Angeles Daily News*.
● The free *LA Weekly* has an excellent listings section.
● Gay-oriented publications include *Frontiers* and *Edge*, which provide listings and entertainment updates.

SENIOR CITIZENS

● Senior citizens discounts are available on a number of services as well as admission to attractions. Take proof of age.
● Inquire ahead for discounts when making reservations for hotels and car rentals.
● Chain restaurants may offer senior citizens discounts on certain menus, and early-bird specials provide savings.
● For information about services and facilities for the elderly at Los Angeles International Airport (LAX), contact Travelers Aid
☎ 310/646-2270

SENSIBLE PRECAUTIONS

- Few visitors ever see LA's high-crime areas, the South-Central district and East LA.
- Venice Beach is unpleasant after dark, infested with drunks and drug peddlers.
- Anybody, particularly lone travelers and women, should be careful and avoid unlit and unpeopled areas after dark.
- Always plan your trip in advance, and consult your car rental agency or hotel staff, or call your destination to confirm the exit you need.
- Do not carry easily snatched bags and cameras.
- Carry only as much cash as you require.
- Don't leave anything of value in cars, even when it is hidden.
- Most hotels provide a safe for valuables. Use it.
- Report lost or stolen items to the nearest police precinct (▷ Lost and Found, 120) if you plan to make a claim.

STUDENT TRAVELERS

- Students with appropriate ID may be entitled to reduced admission to attractions.
- Anyone under 21 may not be allowed into nightclubs.
- To rent a car in California, you must be aged 25 or older.

POPULATION

According to the US Census Bureau, the population of Los Angeles County in 2005 was 9,935,475, up 4.4 percent since 2000. There are more than 2,300 persons per square mile.

Timeline

BEGINNINGS

The Indian village of Yang-Na stood near Los Angeles River, close to the present-day site of City Hall. In 1771 Father Junípèro Serra and Gaspar de Portolá discovered the village and in 1776 founded the Mission of San Gabriel Archangel. Ten years later Los Pobladores, 44 farmer-settlers from the San Gabriel mission, established El Pueblo de Nuestra Señora la Reina de Los Angeles in the fertile Los Angeles basin.

TINSELTOWN

Hollywood and the film industry employed more people in Los Angeles than any other industry in the 1940s. In 1974, the Owens Valley Water Wars were fictionalized in the film *Chinatown*.

1818 The Avila Adobe house, LA's oldest dwelling, is built for cattle rancher and mayor Don Franscico Avila.

1825 California becomes a territory of Mexico.

1842 Gold is discovered in the San Fernando Valley, six years before the discovery at Sutter's Mill that triggered the Gold Rush.

1848 End of the Mexican-American War. California becomes part of the US.

1876 The first transcontinental railway (Southern Pacific) arrives in LA.

1880 The University of Southern California is founded with 53 students.

1881 General Harrison Gray Otis launches the *Los Angeles Times*.

1882 The city's first African-American community is established at 1st and Los Angeles streets.

1892 Oil is discovered Downtown.

1902 Los Angeles' first movie house, the Electric Theater, opens on Main Street. Rose Parade is founded.

1909 Santa Monica Pier opens.

1911 The Nestor Co. founds Hollywood's first movie studio in the Blondeau Tavern at Sunset and Gower.

1913 Cecil B. De Mille makes Hollywood's first full-length feature film, *The Squaw Man*.

1919 The United Artists Film Corp. is founded by D. W. Griffith, Mary Pickford, Douglas Fairbanks and Charlie Chaplin to improve actors' pay and working conditions.

1927 The Academy of Motion Picture Arts and Sciences hosts its first awards ceremony.

1932 The Olympic Games comes to LA. They will return in 1984.

1955 Disneyland opens.

1965 Riots in Watts rage for six days, leaving 34 dead and 1,032 wounded.

1992 Riots follow the acquittal of four white police officers accused of beating black motorist Rodney King.

2003 Frank Gehry's $27 million Walt Disney Concert Hall in Downtown opens, helping to revitalize the area.

2007 Actor, bodybuilder and politician Arnold Schwarzenegger is sworn in for his second term as California's governor.

WATER

As LA boomed around 1900, the demand for water became a major issue. When water bureau superintendent William Mulholland suggested an aqueduct to transport melted snow from the Sierra Nevada to feed the growing city, he was thought to be mad. However, the aqueduct, all 223 miles (359km) and 142 tunnels of it, opened in 1913, and with a 105-mile (169km) extension into the Mono Basin, still serves the city.

NATURAL DISASTERS

Brush fires threatened Malibu in 1993, causing $200 million of damage. In 1994 an earthquake (6.8 on the Richter scale) killed 55 and did $30 billion of damage.

Tiles in El Pueblo de Los Angeles; Avila Adobe on Olvera Street; exhibits in the Los Angeles Times *Building; University of Southern California; lobby of the* Los Angeles Times *Building; Santa Monica Pier (left to right)*

Index

Los Angeles'
25 Best

WRITTEN BY Emma Stanford
ADDITIONAL WRITING BY Julie Jares
DESIGN CONCEPT AND DESIGN WORK Kate Harling
COVER DESIGN Tigist Getachew
INDEXER Marie Lorimer
IMAGE RETOUCHING AND REPRO Michael Moody, Sarah Montgomery and Matt Swann
REVIEWING EDITOR Jacinta O'Halloran
EDITOR Marie-Claire Jefferies
SERIES EDITOR Paul Mitchell

Published in the United Kingdom by AA Publishing

ISBN 978-1-4000-1878-9

FIFTH EDITION

IMPORTANT TIP
Time inevitably brings changes, so always confirm prices, travel facts, and other perishable information when it matters. Although Fodor's cannot accept responsibility for errors, you can use this guide in the confidence that we have taken every care to ensure its accuracy.

SPECIAL SALES
This book is available for special discounts for bulk purchases for sales promotions or premiums. Special editions, including personalized covers, excerpts of existing books, and corporate imprints, can be created in large quantities for special needs. For more information, write to Special Markets/Premium Sales, 1745 Broadway, MD 6–2, New York, NY 10019 or email specialmarkets@randomhouse.com.

Colour separation by Keenes
Printed and bound by Leo, China
10 9 8 7 6 5 4 3 2 1

A03144
Maps in this title produced from map data © Tele Atlas N.V. 2007
Transport map © Communicarta Ltd, UK

The Automobile Association would like to thank the following photographers, companies and picture libraries for their assistance in the preparation of this book.

Abbreviations for the picture credits are as follows – (t) top; (b) bottom; (c) centre; (l) left; (r) right; (AA) AA World Travel Library.

1 AA/M Jourdan; 2/3t AA/P Wood; 4/5t AA/P Wood; 4t AA/C Sawyer; 5 AA/M Jourdan; 6/7t AA/P Wood; 6cl AA/M Jourdan; 6cc AA/M Jourdan; 6cr AA/M Jourdan; 6bl AA/P Wood; 6bc AA/M Jourdan; 6br AA/M Jourdan; 7cl AA/M Jourdan; 7cc AA/M Jourdan; 7cr AA/M Jourdan; 7bl AA/C Sawyer; 7br AA/C Sawyer; 8/9t AA/P Wood; 10/1t AA/P Wood; 10tr AA/M Jourdan; 10cr AA/M Jourdan; 10br AA/P Wood; 10/1b AA/C Sawyer; 11t AA/M Jourdan; 11c AA/C Sawyer; 12/3t AA/P Wood; 13tl AA/M Jourdan; 13ctl Photodisc; 13c Digitalvision; 13bcl AA/P Wood; 13b AA/M Jourdan; 14/5t AA/P Wood; 14tr AA/M Jourdan; 14tcr AA/J Tims; 14bcr AA/M Jourdan; 14br AA/M Jourdan; 16/7t AA/P Wood; 16t AA/C Sawyer; 16tc AA/M Jourdan; 16bc AA/M Jourdan; 16b AA/M Jourdan; 17t © Redfx/ Alamy; 17tc AA/C Sawyer; 17bc AA/C Sawyer; 17b AA/C Sawyer; 18t AA/P Wood; 18tc AA/ M Jourdan; 18c AA/M Jourdan; 18cb AA/C Sawyer; 18b AA/P Wood; 19(I) AA/P Wood; 19(II) AA/P Wood; 19(III) AA/C Sawyer; 19(IV) AA/P Wood; 19(V) AA/C Sawyer; 20/1 AA/M Jourdan; 24l AA/P Wood; 24c AA/M Jourdan; 24r AA/P Wood; 25l AA/M Jourdan; 25r AA/P Wood; 26l AA/M Jourdan; 26r AA/M Jourdan; 27l AA/C Sawyer; 27r AA/P Wood; 28l AA/P Wood; 28/9t AA/M Jourdan; 28br AA/C Sawyer; 29t AA/ C Sawyer; 28/9b AA/P Wood; 29br AA/P Wood; 30tl AA/C Sawyer; 30bl AA/M Jourdan; 30cb AA/M Jourdan; 30br AA/M Jourdan; 30/1t AA/M Jourdan; 30/1b AA/M Jourdan; 31 AA/M Jourdan; 32 AA/C Sawyer; 32/3 AA/C Sawyer; 34/5 Jurassic Park TM & © 2007 Universal Studios, Inc. and Amblin Entertainment, Inc. © 2007 Universal Studios. All Rights Reserved. 35t © 2006 Universal Studios, Inc; 35bl © 2006 Universal Studios, Inc; 35br © 2006 Universal Studios, Inc; 36/7t AA/P Wood; 36bl AA/M Jourdan; 36br AA/M Jourdan; 37bl AA/C Sawyer; 37br AA/M Jourdan; 38t AA/P Wood; 38bl AA/P Wood; 38br AA/P Wood; 39t AA/P Wood; 40t AA/C Sawyer; 41t AA/C Sawyer; 42t AA/C Sawyer; 43t Brand X Pics; 44t Brand X Pics; 45t Brand X Pics; 46/7t AA/J Tims; 48t AA/J Tims; 49 AA/M Jourdan; 52l AA/M Jourdan; 52/3t AA/P Wood; 52/3b AA/P Wood; 53t AA/M Jourdan; 53bl AA/M Jourdan; 53br AA/P Wood; 54tl AA/M Jourdan; 54bl AA/P Wood; 54br AA/P Wood; 54/5t AA/M Jourdan; 55bl AA/M Jourdan; 55r AA/M Jourdan; 56l AA/M Jourdan; 56/7t AA/M Jourdan; 56/7b AA/M Jourdan; 57tr AA/M Jourdan; 57bl AA/P Wood; 57br AA/M Jourdan; 58tl AA/P Wood; 58tc AA/M Jourdan; 58tr AA/P Wood; 59tl AA/M Jourdan; 59tr AA/P Wood; 60/1t AA/P Wood; 60bl AA/M Jourdan; 60br AA/P Wood; 61bl AA/M Jourdan; 61br AA/M Jourdan; 62t AA/P Wood; 63t AA/C Sawyer; 64t Brand X Pics; 65 Photodisc; 66t AA/J Tims; 67 AA/M Jourdan; 70l AA/M Jourdan; 70r AA/M Jourdan; 71tl © 2005 Richard Ross with the courtesy of the J. Paul Getty Trust; 71tr © 2005 Richard Ross with the courtesy of the J. Paul Getty Trust; 72 AA/C Sawyer; 73l AA/C Sawyer; 73r AA/M Jourdan; 74l AA/M Jourdan; 74/5t AA/M Jourdan; 74/5b AA/M Jourdan; 75tr AA/C Sawyer; 75bl AA/C Sawyer; 75bc AA/P Wood; 75br AA/C Sawyer; 76tl AA/P Wood; 76tr AA/P Wood; 77t AA/P Wood; 77bl AA/C Sawyer; 77br AA/M Jourdan; 78t AA/C Sawyer; 79t AA/C Sawyer; 80t AA/C Sawyer; 81t Brand X Pics; 82t Brand X Pics; 83t Corbis; 84t Corbis; 85t AA/J Tims; 86t AA/J Tims; 87 AA/C Sawyer; 90tl AA/P Wood; 90tr AA/P Wood; 91tl AA/C Sawyer; 91tr AA/P Wood; 92l AA/C Sawyer; 92/3t AA/P Wood; 92/3b AA/P Wood; 93t AA/P Wood; 93bl AA/P Wood; 93br AA/P Wood; 94tl AA/C Sawyer; 94tc AA/P Wood; 94tr AA/P Wood; 95t AA/C Sawyer; 95b Brand X Pics; 96t AA/J Tims; 97 AA/C Sawyer; 100l © Disney Enterprises, Inc; 100/1t © Disney Enterprises, Inc; This book makes reference to various Disney copyrighted characters, trademarks, marks and registered marks owned by The Walt Disney Company and Disney Enterprises, Inc. 100/1b © Disney Enterprises, Inc; 101 © Disney Enterprises, Inc and Pixar 102tl AA/C Sawyer; 102tr AA/P Wood; 103tl Rancho Los Alamitos; 103tr Rancho Los Alamitos; 104t AA/P Wood; 104bl PEANUTS © UFS, INC.) © Knott's; 104br AA/C Sawyer; 105 © Knott's; 106t Corbis; 106bl AA/C Sawyer; 106bc AA/C Sawyer; 106br AA/C Sawyer; 107 AA/M Jourdan; 108/9t AA/C Sawyer; 108tr AA; 108tcr AA/M Jourdan; 108bcr AA/M Jourdan; 108br AA/C Sawyer; 110/1t AA/C Sawyer; 112t AA/C Sawyer; 113 AA/M Jourdan; 114/5t AA/M Jourdan; 116/7t AA/M Jourdan; 118/9t AA/M Jourdan; 120/1t AA/M Jourdan; 120b AA/C Sawyer; 122/3t AA/M Jourdan; 123c AA/P Wood; 123b AA/M Jourdan; 124/5t AA/M Jourdan; 124bl AA/P Wood; 124cb AA/P Wood; 124br AA/M Jourdan; 124/5b AA/M Jourdan; 125bl AA/M Jourdan; 125br AA/M Jourdan.

Every effort has been made to trace the copyright holders, and we apologise in advance for any accidental errors. We would be happy to apply the corrections in the following edition of this publication.